New Teeline Dictation Book

About the authors

Doreen Dodds is currently employed by the Northumbria Police Youth Training Scheme; before this she worked at Monkwearmouth College of Further Education. She has considerable experience in writing shorthand examination passages as she is a contributor for the Pitman Examinations Institute.

Sheila Hill had nine years' varied secretarial experience before learning Teeline as her second shorthand system. She is now Chief Examinations Officer and an examiner for Teeline Education Limited.

Hazel Hitchings has extensive business experience in office and secretarial work. She began her teaching career in a South Wales college of further education and is now Head Tutor at Christie Secretarial College, Cheltenham.

Kathleen Tonkin had a successful secretarial career, eventually becoming secretary to the Chief Executive of Rolls Royce (1971) Ltd. In the mid-70s she changed career and took a Certificate of Education. For the last 10 years she has worked full-time in the Department of Business, Management and Computing at Mid-Gloucestershire Technical College.

June Warren worked in further/tertiary education for 29 years teaching the complete range of secretarial subjects. She became Head of School of Secretarial Studies at Colchester Institute and subsequently Head of Secretarial subjects at Yeovil College. She has recently taken early retirement but is now actively working for a number of major examination boards.

Roslyn Willis teaches business and secretarial subjects at New College, Durham and is a BTEC National external examiner in secretarial subjects. Before becoming a full-time lecturer in 1980 Rosalyn had a broad secretarial experience giving her an insight into the work of estate agents, solicitors, building contractors, manufacturing organizations and engineering companies.

NEW TEELINE DICTATION BOOK

Edited by George Hill

Contributors
Doreen Dodds
Sheila Hill
Hazel Hitchings
Kathleen Tonkin
June Warren
Roslyn Willis

HEINEMANN
EDUCATIONAL

Other Teeline titles available

Teeline Shorthand Made Simple by Harry Butler
Teeline Word List by I. C. Hill
Teeline Word Groupings by George Hill and Meriel Bowers
First Teeline Workbook: Revised Edition by I. C. Hill and Meriel Bowers
Second Teeline Workbook: Revised Edition by I. C. Hill and Meriel Bowers
Teeline Shorthand Dictation Passages by Dorothy Bowyer
Teeline Dictation and Drill Book by I. C. Hill and G. S. Hill
Handbook for Teeline Teachers edited by Harry Butler
Medical Teeline by Pat Garner and Pat Clare

Heinemann Educational,
a division of Heinemann Educational Books Ltd
Halley Court, Jordan Hill, Oxford OX2 8EJ

OXFORD   LONDON   EDINBURGH
MELBOURNE   SYDNEY   AUCKLAND
IBADAN   NAIROBI   GABORONE   HARARE
KINGSTON   PORTSMOUTH NH (USA)
SINGAPORE   MADRID

British Library Cataloguing in Publication Data
New Teeline dictation book.
    1. Teeline. Dictation. Questions & answers
I. Hill, George, *1933–*   II. Hill, George *1933–*.
Teeline dictation and drill book
653′.428

    ISBN 0–435–45349–1

Printed in Great Britain by
Richard Clay Ltd, Bungay, Suffolk

Contents

Section Seven **200-word passages**

Section Eight **220-word passages**

Section Nine **240-word passages**

Section Ten **260-word passages**

Preface

The 150 passages in this book have been specially written to provide new speed-building material for Teeline writers. They are word-counted in tens to permit dictation at any required speed, and range in length from 80 words to 360 words; they are suitable for any students who have completed the theory.

The passages have been written by six contributors who are all shorthand teachers or examiners, and this spread of authorship has ensured a variety of topics predominantly, but not exclusively, 'commercial'. They encompass a wide vocabulary, while at the same time providing the repetition of vocabulary necessary for efficient speed-building.

Each passage is preceded by suggested Teeline outlines for selected words or word-groupings, particular attention having been paid to words requiring distinguishing outlines and long words which can be safely abbreviated. In general, the outlines are consistent with those given in other Teeline textbooks, namely *Teeline: revised edition*, *Teeline Shorthand Made Simple*, the *Teeline Word List* and *Teeline Word Groupings*. Occasionally, however, an alternative outline is suggested to improve readability: for instance, the outline ∀ for USUALLY, to remove the danger of mistranscribing ∅ as EASILY ∅ , and vice versa.

No attempt has been made to edit the passages to achieve a pre-set syllabic content; they should therefore prove excellent preparatory material for real work situations and, of course, for Teeline Education Ltd examinations.

Introduction for the teacher

Inserting time-markings

While experienced shorthand teachers may be able to read a word-counted passage at any speed, others may prefer to pencil in time-markings for the required speed. This may be facilitated by referring to the accompanying table, which shows the ordinal positions of the words after which markings should be inserted at quarter-minute intervals. For example, to dictate the first passage in the book at 50 w.p.m., it may be marked as follows:

Dear Madam, Please find enclosed the instruction booklet for the[10] video recorder you ¼ purchased from us last month. I am[20] sorry there has been a ½ delay in sending this to[30] you but our head office was being relocated ¾ during that[40] particular month. Consequently, a backlog of work and a delay[50] 1 in despatching orders has resulted. Should you encounter any difficulties[60] in setting up 1¼ your system, please do not hesitate to[70] contact me and every assistance 1½ will be given. Yours faithfully[80]

The last five words should be read in 6 seconds, making a total of 1 minute 36 seconds' dictation.

Different methods of dictation

Varying the method of dictation can help to solve perennial problems such as classroom boredom (sometimes caused by students being stuck on a speed plateau), and substantial differences between the writing speeds of the fastest and slowest students. The following methods are recommended as useful alternatives to the standard 'constant-speed' dictation.

1. Constant speed with pauses

This method is used to 'stretch' a class and to inspire confidence in their ability to increase speed. For instance, if the class speed is about 50 w.p.m., the chosen passage is marked so that each sentence is read at 60 w.p.m., but with pauses between sentences to make the overall speed only 50 w.p.m. Students should be told to try to speed up towards the end of each sentence, i.e. during the pauses. Example:

Dear Madam, Please find enclosed the instruction booklet for the[10] video recorder you purchased from us last month. *18 secs (4 secs pause)* I am[20] sorry there has been a delay in sending this to[30] you but our head office was

Time intervals in mins. w.p.m.	¼	½	¾	1	1¼	1½	1¾	2	2¼	2½	2¾	3	3¼	3½	3¾	4
40	10	20	30	40	50	60	70	80	90	100	110	120	130	140	150	160
50	12 or 13	25	37 or 38	50	62 or 63	75	87 or 88	100	112 or 113	125	137 or 138	150	162 or 163	175	187 or 188	200
60	15	30	45	60	75	90	105	120	135	150	165	180	195	210	225	240
70	17 or 18	35	52 or 53	70	87 or 88	105	122 or 123	140	157 or 158	175	192 or 193	210	227 or 228	245	262 or 263	280
80	20	40	60	80	100	120	140	160	180	200	220	240	260	280	300	320
90	22 or 23	45	67 or 68	90	112 or 113	135	157 or 158	180	202 or 203	225	247 or 248	270	292 or 293	315	337 or 338	360
100	25	50	75	100	125	150	175	200	225	250	275	300	325	350		
110	27 or 28	55	82 or 83	110	137 or 138	165	192 or 193	220	247 or 248	275	302 or 303	330	357 or 358			
120	30	60	90	120	150	180	210	240	270	300	330	360				
130	32 or 33	65	97 or 98	130	162 or 163	195	227 or 228	260	292 or 293	325	357 or 358					
140	35	70	105	140	175	210	245	280	315	350						
150	37 or 38	75	112 or 113	150	187 or 188	225	262 or 263	300	337 or 338							
160	40	80	120	160	200	240	280	320	360							
170	42 or 43	85	127 or 128	170	212 or 213	255	297 or 298	340								
180	45	90	135	180	225	270	315	360								

being relocated during that[40] particular month.*46 secs (4 secs pause)*
Consequently, a backlog of work and a delay[50] in despatching orders has
resulted.*1 min 3 secs (4 secs pause)* Should you encounter any difficulties[60] in
setting up your system, please do not hesitate to[70] contact me and every
assistance will be given.*1 min 30 secs (4 secs pause)* Yours faithfully[80]
1 min 36 secs (4 secs pause)

2. Increasing speed

This method develops the students' ability to accelerate and to keep
going under pressure. They should be told to carry on writing until
dictation ends, even if their notes are fragmented. Dictation should begin
at the speed of the slowest student and end at 10 w.p.m. faster than the
speed of the fastest student. In this example the passage is marked to be
dictated at 50, 60, 70 and 80 w.p.m. with 20 words to each speed:

Dear Madam, Please find enclosed the instruction booklet for the[10] video
recorder you purchased from us last month. I am[20] *24 secs (4 secs pause)* sorry
there has been a delay in sending this to[30] you but our head office was
being relocated during that[40] *44 secs (4 secs pause)* particular month.
Consequently, a backlog of work and a delay[50] in despatching orders has
resulted. Should you encounter any difficulties[60] *1 min 1 sec (4 secs pause)* in
setting up your system, please do not hesitate to[70] contact me and every
assistance will be given. Yours faithfully[80] *1 min 16 secs (4 secs pause)*

3. Decreasing speed

This method gives slower students an opportunity to write for a short
period at an increased speed and all students to write unhurried accurate
outlines. Students should be told to concentrate on writing neat outlines
and to transcribe their notes immediately after the dictation. Dictation
should begin at the speed of the fastest student and end at 10 w.p.m.
slower than the speed of the slowest student. In this example, the
passage is marked to be dictated at 100, 90, 80 and 70 w.p.m. with 20
words to each speed:

Dear Madam, Please find enclosed the instruction booklet for the[10] video
recorder you purchased from us last month. I am[20] *12 secs (4 secs pause)* sorry
there has been a delay in sending this to[30] you but our head office was
being relocated during that[40] *25 secs (4 secs pause)* particular month.
Consequently, a backlog of work and a delay[50] in despatching orders has
resulted. Should you encounter any difficulties[60] *40 secs (4 secs pause)* in
setting up your system, please do not hesitate to[70] contact me and every
assistance will be given. Yours faithfully[80] *57 secs (4 secs pause)*

4. Shadowing

This method reduces hesitation by the students, thus giving assurance
that they can achieve higher speeds. Use a well-prepared passage and

dictate at a speed comfortable for even the slowest student. Re-dictate at 10 or 20 w.p.m. faster than the original speed, after telling the students to shadow over their original outlines (i.e. they make the necessary movements with pen or pencil but do not actually write). Dictate the passage a third time for shadowing at an even faster speed. Finally, dictate the passage again at the same speed as the third reading, after telling the students to take it down in the normal way (i.e. to write a fresh note of it).

5. Selected outline practice

This method serves to familiarize students with selected outlines that may otherwise cause hesitation during dictation, or mistranscriptions if not accurately written. Select about half a dozen words from the passage you are going to dictate. After allowing a couple of minutes for outline discussion and practice, dictate the words at the target speed, e.g. one word per second if you intend to dictate the passage at 60 w.p.m. Repeat the exercise but change the order in which you dictate the words. Finally, dictate the passage at the target speed.

6. Concentration development

This method serves to test and improve concentration during dictation. Dictate the chosen passage at the average class speed. Ask the best student to read back aloud. The students may now be told – if you wish – that the passage will be re-dictated with some slight changes to the wording. Dictate the passage again at the same speed but with several words altered, e.g. change 'would' to 'will', 'can' to 'could', 'might' to 'may', and so on. Ask another student to read back the passage (again aloud) and all students to see how many of the 'deliberate mistakes' they managed to pick up.

7. Accumulating sprints

This is a good speed- (and confidence-) building method. Choose a passage of between 40 and 80 words or an extract from a longer passage. Divide the passage into 10-word sections. Warn the students that dictation will not necessarily start at the beginning of a sentence or cease at the end of a sentence. Dictate the first 10-word section at the speed of the fastest student, then ask the slowest student to read back aloud and all students to fill in any gaps. Re-dictate at 20 w.p.m. faster. Deal with each 10-word section in the same way until the entire passage has been covered. Complete the exercise by dictating the passage twice, once at the speed of the fastest student, and once at that speed plus 20 w.p.m.

8. Memory development

This method exercises the students' capacity for work retention, thereby helping to reduce tension during dictation. It also provides useful repetition while avoiding the boredom that often accompanies the drilling of single outlines. Tell the students they must not start writing until you tap on your desk or make some other signal. Dictate the first five words at an appropriate speed, then make your signal. When all the students have finished writing, repeat the dictation but add another word. Continue in this way until you judge that most students have reached their limit and have gaps in their notes.

9. Slow dictation

This method provides an opportunity for students to write unhurried (and therefore accurate and readable) outlines during dictation. Dictate the chosen passage at a constant speed, which is 10 w.p.m. below that of the slowest student. Have the passage read back aloud. Re-dictate at a suitable higher speed after telling the students to maintain the standard of their outlines. To provide a challenge for the better students during slow dictation, they may be instructed to write each word as many times as possible or to try new word-groupings.

Note-reading and transcribing

It is not unusual for students and their teachers to become so caught up in the process of writing at ever-increasing speeds, that the skills of note-reading and transcribing are neglected. Quite often the consequence of that neglect is an unexpected examination failure.

A shorthand note that cannot be read is useless: it is therefore appropriate in a book of dictation material to draw the attention of teachers to the importance of devoting adequate classroom time to the development of shorthand reading and transcribing skills. The following notes should prove especially helpful to new shorthand teachers.

1. Taking dictation more or less continually is both mentally and physically tiring. Many teachers believe that the optimum duration of a speed-building session is between 30 and 45 minutes. In practice, however, a teacher may have to cope with a lesson of up to two hours. In such circumstances it is advisable to place the emphasis on dictation in the first hour, and on other activities such as note-reading and outline discussion in the second hour.

2. Every new passage dictated should be either read back or transcribed at least once. 'Getting it down' is only half the battle: the notes must be legible.

3. Class time is precious: reading back is quicker than transcribing and does not tire the writing arm. It also improves fluency and, indirectly, writing speed by imprinting outlines in the mind. Reading back should be done aloud, and the procedure varied between the two extremes of one student reading the whole passage and every student reading a few words in turn.

4. While students are reading back, make a note of any errors or undue hesitation: these are almost always caused by poor outlines requiring remedial action. In particular, be alert to problems associated with common (usually small) words.

5. Do not always have a passage read back immediately after dictating it. Try dictating a passage early in the lesson and have it read back later when the students' memory of it has faded. Good outlines rather than good memory are needed for reading a 'cold note'.

6. Unless students are being taught to produce typed transcripts straight from their shorthand notes, it is not 'cost effective' to make them spend much time transcribing in class. Particularly in the early stages of speed-building, accuracy should take precedence over speed of transcription; the latter will improve as note-reading confidence grows.

7. Transcription exercises in class may be set more often as examination time approaches – assuming the students have reached the required writing speed. The transcription times allowed by different examining bodies can vary considerably, so it is advisable that teachers acquaint themselves accordingly before setting transcription time limits for their students. As a rough guide, however, an allowance of 12 to 15 minutes per 100 words is suggested for handwritten transcripts.

8. Excepting candidates who are entered very prematurely, more examination failures are caused by inaccurate transcribing than by lack of shorthand speed or transcription speed. The most common causes of transcription errors are:
- the careless transcription of correct outlines
- overlooking a section of shorthand notes, often a complete sentence or line
- badly written outlines
- illegible handwriting
- unpunctuated shorthand notes causing incorrect placing of full stops in transcripts

Students should be trained always to check carefully through a completed transcript, preferably twice. The first check should be made with reference to the shorthand notes to pick up any outlines wrongly transcribed, or simply overlooked during transcription. The second check should be a straight reading of the transcript to ensure that it makes sense; if not, then the shorthand notes should be checked yet again. Finally, time permitting, if the length of the passage is known to them, students should count the words in their transcript; if short of the required total, the odd outline may still have been overlooked.

9. Very rarely, if ever, is the working shorthand writer – not to mention the examination candidate – required to read or transcribe notes written by someone else. Consequently, making students do this in class is far less productive than reading or transcribing their own notes. This is especially so where Teeline is the system and students are being taught, in essence, how to reduce their own handwriting rather than to master a completely different written language. Therefore, although

reading printed outlines may be helpful while learning the theory of any system, its value decreases rapidly as speed-building progresses. To bring variety (even hilarity) into a lesson, the students may be asked occasionally to exchange notes for reading back or transcription, but this will not help students to read their own notes fluently.

Section One
80-word passages

1 A letter about a missing instruction booklet

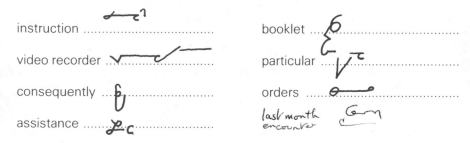

instruction ....

booklet ....

video recorder ....

particular ....

consequently ....

orders ....

assistance ....

last month
encounter

Dear Madam, Please find enclosed the <u>instruction</u> <u>booklet</u> for the[10] <u>video</u> <u>recorder</u> you purchased from us <u>last month</u>. I am[20] sorry there has been a delay in sending this to[30] you but our <u>head office</u> was being relocated during that[40] <u>particular</u> month. <u>Consequently</u>, a backlog of work and a delay[50] in despatching <u>orders</u> has resulted. Should you <u>encounter</u> any difficulties[60] in setting up your system, please do not hesitate to[70] contact me and every <u>assistance</u> will be given. Yours faithfully[80]

2 Skin care

routine ....

moisturize ....

regularly ....

overnight ....

unsightly ....

blemished ....

important

Skin care should be an <u>important</u> part of your daily[10] <u>routine</u>. The experts tell us to cleanse, tone and <u>moisturize</u>.[20] If the skin is not cared for and cleansed <u>regularly</u>,[30] spots are often the result. The worst crime you can[40] <u>commit</u> is to leave make-up on <u>overnight</u>. This clogs[50] up the pores of the skin and can lead to[60] <u>unsightly</u> sores. When our skin is blemished we do not[70] look our best and, therefore, do not feel our best.[80]

3 A notice asking members to notify any change of address

address

informed	membership
records	remember
necessary	clearly
up to date	

Please note that it is very <u>important</u> to keep us[10] <u>informed</u> of any change of <u>address</u> that you have made,[20] or are about to make. This is the only way[30] that we can be sure that our <u>membership records</u> are[40] <u>completely</u> <u>up to date</u>. Complete the card with your new[50] address and your membership number. <u>Remember</u> to include your post[60] code and then send the card to us. It is[70] not <u>necessary</u> to use a stamp. Please print very <u>clearly</u>.[80]

4 A letter returning an incorrect invoice

invoice	errors
overcharged	refund
this letter	

Dear Sir, I have received your <u>invoice</u> for the books[10] I <u>ordered</u> from you. I am returning this to you,[20] as it contains two <u>errors</u>. You have <u>overcharged</u> me for[30] the cookery book. The price is ten pounds but the[40] <u>invoice</u> shows this as twelve pounds. Also, I did not[50] order the <u>gardening</u> book which is listed on the invoice.[60] Please correct these <u>errors</u> and <u>refund</u> the cost of the[70] stamp I have used to send this letter. Yours faithfully[80]

5 A special offer on new cars

draw your attention	maximum
trade-in	coupled
interest-free	

Dear Customer, It is several years now since you purchased[10] your last car from us and we would like to[20] draw your attention to a special offer we are making[30] on new cars during the month of April. For this[40] month only we are offering maximum trade-in prices coupled[50] with interest-free loans on our new cars. We do[60] not think you can afford to miss such a generous[70] offer, so please come and see us soon. Yours faithfully[80]

6 Training courses in word processing

companies ...... *Ce* ......

word processors ......

performance ...... *Vce MSe* ......

under-use ......

short-sighted ...... *S* ......

offset ......

technology ......

more + more

More and more companies are buying word processors, as their[10] performance improves and their price decreases. Most firms have some[20] system of training operators, but some expect typists to pick[30] up a knowledge of word processing as they go along.[40] This leads to the under-use of the equipment and[50] is a short-sighted policy since the cost of sending[60] staff on training courses will be offset by the more[70] efficient use that can be made of the new technology.[80]

7 A personal letter about a new house

above address ......

in order to be ......

get away ......

Christmas ......

Dear Mary, You will be pleased to learn that since[10] my last letter to you, Tom and I have moved[20] to the above address. We sold our house and bought[30] this cottage in the country in order to be near[40] our son and his family. You must come and visit[50] us when you are able to get away from your[60] business. Perhaps you could stay for a few days at[70] Christmas? I look forward to hearing from you. Yours, Janet[80]

8 A letter confirming a hotel booking

thank you for your letter ....   I am pleased ....

publicity ....   leaflet ....

arrangement ....

Dear Sir, Thank you for your letter enquiring about accommodation[10] at
this hotel. I am pleased to be able to[20] offer you the rooms you require on
the 14th and[30] 15th of June and enclose with this letter a publicity[40]
leaflet. I note that your party will be arriving in[50] the early evening and
confirm this arrangement. My staff and[60] I look forward to welcoming
your party to our hotel[70] and thank you for your booking. Yours
faithfully, Hotel Manager[80]

9 Students' union notice about blood-donor session

blood transfusion

transfusion ....   union ....

worthwhile ....   unit ....

departmental ....   enrolment ....

There have been many offers from students willing to give[10] blood to the
blood-transfusion service. The students' union is[20] trying to raise support
to make it worth while for[30] a blood-transfusion unit to visit the college.
The unit[40] will be located in the main hall for one whole[50] day as this is
the most suitable venue. If you[60] would like to give blood, please contact
your departmental union[70] representative or complete an enrolment
form available from this office.[80]

10 A personal letter from Margaret to Ruth

especially ....   celebrate ....

absolutely ....   certainly ....

Margaret ....

Dear Ruth, It was lovely to see you again after[10] such a long time and especially to celebrate your marriage[20] to Ian. The whole day went very well and you[30] looked absolutely lovely. Ian is a most charming man and[40] I am sure you will both have a very happy[50] life together. I have arranged to take a week's holiday[60] at the end of next month and shall certainly call[70] to see you both. With lots of love from Margaret[80]

Section Two
100-word passages

1 A memo about training courses

organization ...... *(shorthand)* ......   appropriate ...... *(shorthand)* ......

secretarial ...... *(shorthand)* ......   envisage ...... *(shorthand)* ......

preference ...... *(shorthand)* ......

The company has recently decided to install word processors throughout[10] the organization. We are planning appropriate training courses for secretarial[20] staff, with up to eight places on each course. We[30] envisage one course per week, the first to commence on[40] 10th May. Bearing in mind the need to retain cover[50] at a time when some of your staff may be[60] away on holiday, could you please submit lists of trainees[70] with your preference for any particular week's course for the[80] period 10th May to 26th July. Please use the[90] reference numbers on the attached slip when compiling your lists.[100]

2 Notes from an annual general meeting

balanced ...... *(shorthand)* ......   economic ...... *(shorthand)* ......

achievement ...... *(shorthand)* ......   workforce ...... *(shorthand)* ......

continuing ...... *(shorthand)* ......

Following the annual general meeting I am pleased to inform[10] all concerned that our books have not only balanced, but[20] we have had a rise in profits of some thirty[30] per cent. In today's economic climate this is no small[40] achievement and the chairman wishes to express his thanks to[50] the entire workforce for their efforts over the past year.[60] After the very poor results obtained during the previous financial[70] year, it is a relief to see our company back[80] in a strong trading position. By continuing with our policy[90] of expansion we can approach the coming year with confidence.[100]

3 The quantity and quality of magazines

amazing .... ～ゔ, ...

(amusing .... ～ゔ/ ....)

specialized ....𝒫 ....

(specialist ....𝒫 ....)

usually ....

glossy ....

illustrations ... .

The variety of magazines on sale in the shops is[10] quite amazing. There must be hundreds, if not thousands, to[20] choose from. Most age groups and interests are well catered[30] for. Choices can be made from general-interest items to[40] specialized subjects such as financial management. The content of the[50] magazines seems to improve with each passing year and the[60] quality of the paper on which they are printed is[70] usually very high, being of the thick glossy kind. In[80] addition, the quality of the photographs and other illustrations seems[90] to have improved by leaps and bounds in recent years.[100]

4 A letter asking Mr Roberts to be a guest speaker

kindly ....

remarked ....

wondering ....

fee ....

Dear Mr Roberts, You may remember that you kindly visited[10] this society in March last year and gave a talk[20] on your travels in China. All our members remarked on[30] how interesting they found this talk and it was certainly[40] one of the most popular we have ever had. We[50] are just arranging our meeting for this year and we[60] are wondering whether you would be able to return and[70] talk on the same subject, perhaps telling us all about[80] your second trip to China. We should, of course, pay[90] all your expenses plus the usual small fee. Yours sincerely[100]

5 A report about pupils winning a Highway Code competition

highway ......

police ......

contest ......

answer ......

filmed ......

Friday night ......

A team of five young pupils from our local school[10] has won the Highway Code competition run by the county's[20] police force. Forty schools from all over the county took[30] part and just three teams were left to compete in[40] the final. It was a difficult contest, but our team[50] had done their homework well and they were able to[60] answer almost all the questions. They each received a prize[70] of five pounds and also a set of posters for[80] the school. The contest was filmed, and part of it[90] will be shown on local television news on Friday night.[100]

6 A letter about an accounting error

overdrawn ......

automatically ......

deposit account ......

current account ......

insufficient ......

Dear Sir, I was very surprised to note from my[10] bank statement that I am overdrawn by the sum of[20] one hundred and ten pounds and I feel there must[30] be some mistake. You will recall that I made an[40] arrangement with your branch to transfer money automatically from my[50] deposit account to my current account as the latter became[60] low. This system has worked well for the past five[70] years and I cannot believe that there are insufficient funds[80] in my deposit account to prevent transfer to the current[90] account. Please look into this matter without delay. Yours faithfully[100]

7 Opening a bank account

likely ......

(luckily ......)

frequently ......

withdraw ......

whichever ......

career ......

When you start work it is very likely that you[10] will be paid by cheque. This will mean that you[20] need to open a current account at a bank. You[30] will have to decide on the bank and the branch[40] at which to open your account. Many young people use[50] the same bank as their parents. Some decide on the[60] one which their company uses since they have to visit[70] it frequently to bank money or withdraw petty cash. Whichever[80] one you decide on, it is likely that you will[90] stay with that bank for the rest of your career.[100]

8 A letter to a customer about repairs to a cooker

engineer

apologize

as soon as

inconvenience

Dear Mrs White, We thank you for your letter of[10] yesterday's date and are sorry to learn about the problems[20] you are having with your cooker. I have contacted Mr[30] Green, the engineer who has been repairing your cooker, and[40] he assures me that the parts needed are on order[50] and are expected within seven days. As soon as these[60] are received we will be contacting you again in order[70] to arrange for Mr Green to call at your home.[80] We apologize for any inconvenience you have been caused whilst[90] your cooker has been out of service. Yours sincerely, Manager[100]

9 A letter from a customer about a faulty cooker

I was pleased

state of affairs

greatly

unfortunately

unsatisfactory

appreciated

Dear Sir, I thank you for your letter concerning the[10] problems with my cooker. I was pleased to hear that[20] you expect the latest fault to be repaired when the[30] parts arrive and that your service engineer will be able[40] to undertake the repair. Unfortunately, it is now ten days[50] after the date of your letter and I have still[60] not heard from Mr Green. I have now been unable[70] to prepare a cooked meal for my family for five[80] weeks and consider this state of affairs to be most[90] unsatisfactory. Your early comments would be greatly appreciated. Yours faithfully[100]

10 A letter regarding double-glazing

double-glazed ....   installed ......

straight away ....   courteous .....

recommend ....

Dear Sir, This is just a short note to let[10] you know how very pleased I am with the double-[20] glazed windows your company installed in my house last week.[30] The workmen arrived on time and began working straight away.[40] Great care was taken not to damage any decorations or[50] furnishings and dust sheets were placed over carpets. The windows[60] have been fitted to a very high standard. The two[70] workmen were courteous throughout the day and are a credit[80] to your company. I shall certainly recommend your company very[90] highly to my friends and relations. Yours truly, Christine Hardy[100]

Section Three
120-word passages

1 Housekeeping in the office

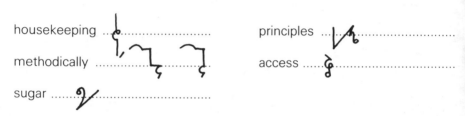

housekeeping ....

methodically ....

sugar ....

principles ....

access ....

What is housekeeping? In the home the term refers to[10] looking after the house and keeping it clean and tidy.[20] It also means careful budgeting and making the best use[30] of what you have available. When the term housekeeping is[40] used in the office, the same basic principles should apply.[50] For instance, when creating a new document on a word[60] processor, it will need a file name. Great care should[70] be taken to name the document sensibly using some sort[80] of logical method. If the naming of the document is[90] not carried out methodically it may be difficult to access[100] it at a later date – rather like looking for sugar[110] which has been stored in a coffee jar, in fact.[120]

2 A letter about a fashion show preview

next Friday ....

cordially ....

pleasant ....

established ....

free of charge ....

Dear Madam, Next Friday our store is holding a fashion[10] show which will enable us to give customers a preview[20] of the styles which will be on sale next season.[30] As an established account holder you are cordially invited to[40] attend. You will find enclosed two free tickets, so please[50] feel free to bring along a guest. Cheese and wine[60] will be served free of charge during the course of[70] the evening, so a pleasant time should be had by[80] all. Should any particular garment appeal to you, dressing rooms[90] will be available for use, together with help from staff.[100] We look forward to seeing you and your guest, if[110] you feel the evening would be of interest. Yours faithfully[120]

3 Safety advice for cyclists

bicycle ....   basic ....

reflective ....

If you ride a bicycle, there are a few basic[10] rules that you must remember. Always watch out for careless[20] drivers, especially when you are riding in towns. A lot[30] of drivers cut corners, which makes it very dangerous for[40] the cyclist. You must not change lanes suddenly and you[50] must not weave in and out of slow-moving traffic.[60] If you go out on your bike at night, your[70] front and rear lights must be kept in good working[80] order. It is a good idea to wear a reflective[90] arm band or jacket to ensure you can be seen[100] easily. Always give clear hand signals and make them in[110] good time, and do not go too fast down hills.[120]

4 A letter of thanks for a lunch

to say ....   excellent ....

interested ....   project ....

proposals ....

Dear Bob, This is just to say how much we[10] enjoyed meeting you and Mary yesterday and to thank you[20] for the excellent lunch. It seems amazing that it is[30] two years since we last met and there was certainly[40] a lot of news to catch up on. I was[50] very interested to hear of your project and I will[60] take the matter up with my chairman when I return[70] to work next week. I think he will want to[80] put your proposals to the Board when it next meets,[90] and I shall hope to have some good news for[100] you after that. Jane sends her best wishes to Mary.[110] She will be writing in a few days. Yours sincerely[120]

5 A letter of thanks for an office tour

I am writing ....

sincerely ....

employers ....

grateful ....

demonstrated ....

Dear Mrs Bright, I am writing to thank you most[10] sincerely for showing my students and me around your offices[20] last Wednesday. We found our visit most interesting and we[30] really do appreciate the trouble you went to in order[40] to make it so worthwhile. We have to rely on[50] the goodwill of local employers for showing our students the[60] latest office technology. We do not have a telex or[70] fax machine at college for them to see, and the[80] equipment in your mail room is very modern, too. The[90] students enjoyed the tour very much and learned a great[100] deal from it. We are most grateful to you, and[110] all your staff who demonstrated equipment to us. Yours sincerely[120]

6 A memo to staff regarding fire drills

shortly ....

personal possessions ....

assemble ....

quietly ....

effectiveness ....

Will you please note that a fire drill will be[10] held shortly. Staff should acquaint themselves with their nearest escape[20] route and follow this on the sounding of the fire[30] siren. Remember to close office doors if possible but not[40] if, in so doing, you would put yourself at risk.[50] Do not go back for personal possessions. Walk quietly and[60] quickly but do not push. Staff should assemble on the[70] front lawn, and wait until a roll is called before[80] returning to their offices. Fire monitors have been appointed for[90] each floor to check that there is no one left[100] in the building. A report will be issued later on[110] the effectiveness of the drill, recommending new procedures where necessary.[120]

7 The Woodlands Trust

wildlife ......   countryside ......

activities ......   habitat ......

unusual ......   at the same time ......

We often read about the need to protect the wildlife[10] and countryside of Britain, but not many people know about[20] the charity known as the Woodlands Trust. The Trust has[30] been set up to conserve woodland in Britain and to[40] do this it buys woods to protect; also, land on[50] which to establish new woodland. These activities help to conserve[60] the habitat of wild animals and birds and create quiet[70] places which people can enjoy. A popular service offered by[80] the Trust, for a small fee, is the planting of[90] a tree in someone's name. Many people do this as[100] an unusual and rather special present which, at the same[110] time, helps to preserve this country's heritage for future generations.[120]

8 A personal letter from Beryl to David

invitation ......   reputation ......

crown ......   kindest ......

Dear David, It was lovely to hear from you again[10] and to know that you and Janet are enjoying your[20] stay in this country. I appreciate your kind invitation to[30] have dinner with you both on the 14th in the[40] Royal Hotel, but unfortunately I shall be away on business[50] on that date. However, I shall be back in the[60] country on the 17th so perhaps we could meet then?[70] In answer to your enquiry about accommodation in York, I[80] know that the Crown Inn has a good reputation and,[90] although I have not stayed there, I have friends who[100] recommend it. Do let me know if you wish me[110] to make a booking for you. With kindest regards, Beryl[120]

9 A letter requesting an article for a magazine

last summer ....   we were pleased ....

picnics ....   similarly ....

inclusion ....   seasonal ....

contributions ....

Dear Mr Hastings, Last summer we were pleased to publish[10] a humorous article by you entitled 'Picnics in the Rain',[20] and we wonder if you would be willing to write[30] a similarly humorous article for inclusion in the special Christmas[40] edition of this magazine? We require a piece of about[50] eight hundred words on a seasonal topic such as office[60] parties or food and drink. Payment will be on acceptance[70] and in the region of sixty pounds, depending on the[80] exact number of words. We plan to publish the magazine[90] during the first week of December, so all contributions must[100] be in our hands by the last day of October.[110] Please let us know if you can oblige. Yours sincerely[120]

10 A letter about possible legal action

self-explanatory ....   incident ....

strongly ....   course of action ....

Dear Miss Curtis, I enclose a copy of a letter[10] received today from Messrs Williams and Thompson, the contents of[20] which are self-explanatory. I find it very hard to[30] believe that they are unable to bring this matter to[40] a happy conclusion, and would appreciate your comments on their[50] letter before I reply fully to them. I would point[60] out, however, that as it is now eight weeks since[70] this incident was first brought to their attention, we would[80] be in a good position to take this case to[90] the County Court. I strongly advise you to consider this[100] course of action as it may be the only way[110] to resolve the matter. Kind regards, Yours sincerely, Kate Brown[120]

Section Four
140-word passages

1 Leisure centre facilities

facilities ....   gymnastics ....

trampolining ....   from the beginning ....

table-tennis ....   citizens ....

In this city four leisure centres have been built over[10] the past ten years. These centres provide excellent facilities for[20] those who wish to raise their standard in their favourite[30] sport, or are interested in taking up a new sport.[40] The opening hours are from seven-thirty a.m. to ten-[50]forty p.m., seven days a week. Special classes are arranged[60] for children, such as swimming and gymnastics, while adults can[70] choose from keep-fit, body-conditioning and trampolining. Racquet games[80] such as tennis, squash and badminton can be played throughout[90] the day, but courts do have to be booked twenty-[100]four hours in advance. From the beginning of next month[110] bowls and table-tennis are being organized for senior citizens[120] and the less energetic members of our city. There is[130] something for everyone at these centres at very reasonable charges.[140]

2 A letter about a riding club meeting

Dear Sir or Madam ....   replacing ....

badly ....   organized ....

castle ....

Dear Sir or Madam, We have much pleasure in informing[10] you that the next meeting of the Riding Club will[20] be held on Saturday, 14th July at two-thirty p.m.[30] at the Park Community Centre. We hope you will make[40] an effort to be present at this meeting as we[50] have many important matters to discuss. We also have to[60] discuss the best way to raise money for repairing and[70] replacing our show jumps. Many of these were badly damaged[80] during the summer shows and will have to be repaired[90] in time for the next season. We have organized the[100] Summer Ball to be held at the Castle Hotel on[110] Friday, 1st August. Tickets are in the process of being[120] printed and will be on sale at the July meeting[130] at a cost of seven pounds each. Yours faithfully, Secretary[140]

3 A letter about an appointment for an eye test

appointment

optician

emigrated

Australia

ophthalmics

administered

Dear Mrs Parks, I am writing to let you know[10] that an appointment has been arranged for you to have[20] your yearly eye test on Friday, 10th September. Please bring[30] with you the spectacles normally worn for reading. The optician[40] who usually conducts your eye test is, unfortunately, no longer[50] with us. He and his family have emigrated to Australia.[60] However, he has been replaced by Mr Black, who has[70] an excellent reputation and much experience in the field of[80] ophthalmics. We strongly recommend that you leave your car at[90] home when you attend the appointment. This is because the[100] eye drops administered cause the vision to blur for up[110] to three hours. Under these circumstances, driving a car would[120] be very unsafe and could lead to an accident. Perhaps[130] you could arrange for someone to accompany you. Yours sincerely[140]

4 Enjoying the countryside

serenity

as well as

magnificent

scents

scenery

scant

Do you enjoy walking? There are many people who do,[10] especially in the countryside. A great sense of peace and[20] serenity can be found in the countryside, as well as[30] a thousand and one things to see and hear. Try[40] sitting under the shade of an old oak tree and[50] listen to the singing of the large variety of birds.[60] Open your eyes and do not just glance, but really[70] absorb the beauty that surrounds you. Take in the magnificent[80] array of plant life. Observe the many shades and colours,[90] and the delightful scents that emanate from the flowers. Too[100] many of us take for granted the surrounding scenery. We[110] look without really seeing, paying scant attention to the wonders[120] that nature provides. The sights and sounds are free for[130] all to enjoy at any time, winter and summer alike.[140]

5 A letter from a college to a firm about a display of office equipment

display .... 𝑒 ....   take part .... 𝒱 ....

great interest ..... 𝒥___𝑒 ....   as soon as possible .... 𝑜𝑝 ....

Dear Sirs, We shall be holding our annual display of[10] office equipment again this year, and we are hoping that[20] you will wish to take part as you have in[30] the past. As you know, this display has always proved[40] to be of great interest to the students and we[50] are sure that they act as good representatives for you[60] when they get out to work. We know of several[70] purchases that have been made by companies because their office[80] staff have spoken well of a particular brand. The display[90] will take place in the main hall of the college[100] and will be held on Tuesday, 5th July. We do[110] hope you will be able to come along, and, if[120] so, could you let us know as soon as possible[130] the amount of floor space you will need. Yours faithfully[140]

6 Details of a library service for a new member

library .... 𝐿 ....   suit .... 𝑒𝑟 ....

in the morning ..... 𝐿 ....

We are pleased to welcome you as a new member[10] of the library. Your card is enclosed and you should[20] sign it immediately in the blank space. Keep it in[30] a safe place as you will need to bring it[40] with you each time you come to select your books.[50] The library has a very wide range of books and[60] we think we have something to suit all tastes. If[70] you cannot find a particular book you want, please ask[80] at the desk. If it is in our stock, we[90] can reserve it for you. If it is not on[100] our lists, we may be able to get it for[110] you from another library. We are open each day except[120] Sunday from ten in the morning until four in the[130] afternoon, and also on Tuesday evening from six until nine.[140]

7 A letter about an unsatisfactory service on a car

complain ....

dissatisfied ....

renewal ....

misfire ....

very soon ....

incorrectly ....

additional expenses ....

Dear Sirs, I write to complain about the recent service[10] your garage carried out on my car. I have used[20] your garage ever since I bought my car from you,[30] and this is the first time I have been dissatisfied[40] with the service provided. The latest service was a major[50] one and should have covered renewal of the plugs and[60] checking of the points. However, the car started to misfire[70] very soon after I collected it from you and I[80] had to call for roadside assistance. The engineer showed me[90] the plugs; they were black and had obviously not been[100] renewed. He also said the points were set incorrectly. It[110] seems to me that something has gone wrong in your[120] Service Department, and I anticipate receiving an offer from you[130] to compensate for my inconvenience and additional expenses. Yours faithfully[140]

8 A letter about fitting caravan windows

very well ....

scale drawing ....

exactly ....

inserted ....

feasibility ....

Dear Sirs, I have to come to Yorkshire on business[10] next month and I am wondering whether this would be[20] a good opportunity for you to fit the windows in[30] my motor caravan. You said it would take you two[40] days, and this would fit in very well with my[50] visit. I have prepared a scale drawing showing exactly where[60] the windows are to be inserted, and enclose this for[70] your comments. You know the structure of the vehicle concerned[80] and will be able to advise on the feasibility of[90] cutting in the proposed positions. When you have had time[100] to study my plan, perhaps you would be kind enough[110] to ring me on the number above so that we[120] may make an appointment. I shall be available most days,[130] and I look forward to hearing from you. Yours faithfully[140]

9 A letter of complaint from a hotel to a laundrette

telephone conversation .... laundry ....

your company .... together with ....

compensation ....

Dear Sirs, I confirm my telephone conversation with your secretary[10] when I complained that the laundry your company delivered to[20] us yesterday was unable to be accepted by our housekeeper.[30] The faults she found upon checking the linen were as[40] follows: fifteen of the thirty double sheets were torn; seventeen[50] white bath towels were stained red; six sets of white[60] pillow cases were missing, together with three double blankets; and [70] only six of the twenty aprons were returned. I am[80] sure you will agree that this situation is unsatisfactory, and[90] if we are to continue to ask your company to[100] provide a laundry service I shall expect to receive either[110] replacements or compensation for the damaged and lost items. This[120] settlement must be reached before your next laundry collection on[130] Saturday. Please let me have your early comments. Yours faithfully[140]

10 A memo from a hotel manager

boardroom .... assistant chef ....

vacancy .... at the present time ....

There will be a monthly meeting of all department managers[10] on Friday, 6th June at 10 a.m. in the boardroom.[20] The agenda for the meeting has already been circulated but[30] there are two points to which I particularly wish to[40] draw your attention. Item five concerns the appointment of an[50] assistant chef and I would like you to give some[60] thought to the question of where we should advertise this[70] vacancy, together with the job description. I have already discussed[80] this matter with the head chef and we have in[90] mind a minimum age of twenty-five, but would welcome[100] your views. Item three refers to our celebrations in July[110] to mark the hotel's first birthday. As you have all[120] been working on this project, please bring with you all[130] the information you have on file at the present time.[140]

Section Five
160-word passages

1 Car-maintenance classes

maintenance .... newspaper ....

consisted .... problem ....

I seemed to be spending a lot of money at[10] my local garage on simple maintenance jobs to my car,[20] such as changing the oil and replacing light bulbs. I[30] was quite delighted when I read in the newspaper of[40] evening classes in car maintenance being held at my local[50] college. I enrolled at once. How surprised I was to[60] discover that over half the class consisted of females! I[70] have now attended four lessons and enjoyed every minute of[80] them. I now know how an engine works and I[90] can change the oil, the light bulbs, the plugs and[100] the tyres. If my car will not start in damp[110] weather, I no longer have to abandon it and catch[120] a bus, and if the battery is flat I know[130] how to recharge it. My only problem now is my[140] husband phoning me for help when his car breaks down[150] or a tyre bursts on his way home from work.[160]

2 A letter about damaged luggage

insurance .... subsequent ....

inevitable .... mutually ....

telephone number ....

Dear Miss Johnson, I am in receipt of your insurance[10] claim for the damage caused to your suitcase and the[20] subsequent loss of contents. Firstly, may I apologize for the[30] damage to your suitcase. Although my staff take as much[40] care as possible when loading luggage on to the aircraft,[50] it is inevitable that occasional accidents will happen. With regard[60] to the loss of several items from the suitcase, I[70] would ask you to make a list, itemizing the lost[80] contents. I would then like to arrange an appointment to[90] see you so that an official claim can be lodged.[100] Please could you telephone me so that a mutually convenient[110]date and time can be arranged. You will find my[120] telephone number at the bottom of this letter. May I[130] apologize for any inconvenience you have been caused and assure[140] you of my best attention at all times. Yours sincerely,[150] George Brown, telephone number: Tyneside 31975.[160]

3 The value of regular exercise

strenuous ....

destination ....

temptation ....

it goes without saying ....

Medical experts tell us that regular exercise is important to[10] the maintenance of good health, but there are many people[20] who shudder at the thought of strenuous exercise. Others claim[30] they do not have the time to devote to regular[40] exercise. This need not be the case. Try walking to[50] work or college instead of catching the bus. If the[60] distance from home to work is too great, then try[70] getting off the bus one or two stops before your[80] destination and walk the rest of the way. When you[90] arrive at work or college try to resist the temptation[100] to use the lift and walk up the stairs instead.[110] Of course, taking regular exercise is only a part of[120] keeping fit. A healthy and balanced diet is at least[130] as important. Also, it goes without saying that those who[140] smoke or drink to excess will never achieve full fitness,[150] even if they do eat sensibly and take regular exercise.[160]

4 An application for the post of shorthand-typist with a newspaper

audio-typing ....

solicitor's ....

(selector's ....)

Dear Sirs, I have seen your advertisement in the local[10] paper for a shorthand-typist to work with your company,[20] and I am very interested in the post you are[30] offering. I am nineteen years of age and I left[40] college two years ago after passing examinations in advanced typewriting[50] and shorthand at one hundred and twenty words a minute.[60] I also studied office practice, audio-typing and word processing.[70] Since then I have been working as a typist in[80] a solicitor's office where my duties include meeting the general[90] public and operating a computer. I enjoy this work and[100] feel that I have gained a great deal of useful[110] experience during the two years I have been there. However,[120] I do not use my shorthand and I want to[130] find a job where this skill would be useful. I[140] am also keen to work on the staff of a[150] newspaper. I look forward to hearing from you. Yours faithfully[160]

5 An advertisement for a sales manager for a safety-equipment company

international ....

rapidly ....

candidates ....

background ....

above all ....

Our company is part of a large international group based[10] in Britain. We produce safety equipment which is used in[20] industries such as mining and deep-sea diving. We have[30] expanded rapidly over the last two or three years and[40] we are now looking for a sales manager. Candidates should[50] have an electrical background and should have several years' experience[60] of selling in this area. Above all, we need someone[70] with plenty of ideas and with the drive and energy[80] to introduce new customers to the firm. He or she[90] will also be expected to encourage the sales force to[100] achieve even higher sales. The post will be based in[110] the south-west of the country, and will include an[120] excellent salary and a company car. We are prepared to[130] assist with the expense of moving if required. There is[140] a good pension scheme and various other benefits. Telephone the[150] personnel officer on the above number for an application form.[160]

6 A letter of complaint about an insurance policy

insurance company ....

last Friday ....

blood pressure ....

premium ....

Dear Sirs, I wish to complain very strongly about the[10] service I have received from your insurance company. To begin[20] with, you assured me on the telephone that I would[30] be covered as from last Friday, but on Monday when[40] you had received the proposal form you rang to say[50] that you could not accept me on your Mature Drivers'[60] policy as I have to take one tablet a day[70] for raised blood pressure. I feel I need not have[80] declared this fact, since with the medication my health is[90] excellent and there must be many people insured by you[100] who have never had their blood pressure tested. I am[110] not prepared to pay the extra premium you now require[120] and should be grateful if you would return my evidence[130] of no claims' discount which I sent with my proposal[140] form. I am not impressed with the service received, and[150] hope you will take note of this fact. Yours faithfully[160]

7 A walking holiday

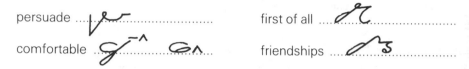

persuade ....   first of all ....

comfortable ....   friendships ....

Have you ever considered spending your annual holiday on a[10] walking tour? If not, then I may be able to[20] persuade you what great pleasure can be obtained from exploring[30] on your own two feet. First of all, there is[40] much fun to be derived from planning the route. It[50] is very important not to try to cover too much[60] distance on your first trip, and also to get fit[70] before you start. Then you must collect your equipment, making[80] sure you have comfortable boots and really waterproof clothing. You[90] may decide to stay overnight at hostels, which keeps down[100] the cost and introduces you to others who are enjoying[110] the open air. Many lasting friendships are made whilst exchanging[120] stories of the day's events around the dinner table. You[130] will soon learn to read a map and discover for[140] yourself the most interesting places to visit on your tour.[150] Do try it and discover the fun to be had![160]

8 A letter about evening classes

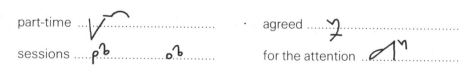

part-time ....   agreed ....

sessions ....   for the attention ....

Dear Mrs Brown, Our records for last term show that[10] you were a student in a cookery evening class, and[20] that you enquired if there was to be a similar[30] class held in the future. At that time we were[40] not certain that we would be able to hold further[50] evening classes, but we are now pleased to inform you[60] that we have recently secured the services of Miss Newton,[70] a part-time teacher, who has agreed to take classes[80] from 13th April until 10th June. These sessions will last[90] from seven p.m. until nine p.m. and the title of[100] the course will be 'Cooking on a Budget'. If you[110] are interested in this course, the fee for which will[120] be fifteen pounds, please complete the enclosed application form and[130] return it to the Home Economics Department to arrive not[140] later than the end of this month. Please mark it[150] for the attention of Mrs Hope. Yours sincerely, James Cross[160]

9 A letter supplying a reference

intermediate ....

relationship ....

perform ....

forthcoming ....

punctual ....

Dear Sirs, Thank you for your letter of 16th March[10] asking for a reference for Miss Janet Green, who has[20] applied for the post of shorthand-typist with your firm.[30] Janet has been a student at this college on the[40] two-year secretarial course which ends on 20th June. During[50] her time with us she has gained examination passes in[60] shorthand, typewriting and office skills at intermediate level, and is[70] taking these subjects at advanced level in the forthcoming examinations.[80] Her tutors expect her to gain credits in all subjects.[90] She has proved to be a popular member of her[100] group and has always had a good relationship with her[110] teachers. She is a punctual and hard-working student and[120] I have no hesitation in recommending her for the post[130] you describe, as I consider she has the ability to[140] perform her duties to your complete satisfaction. Please let me[150] know if you require any more information. Yours faithfully, Principal[160]

10 An account of a road accident

version ....

postman ....

passenger seat ....

ambulance ....

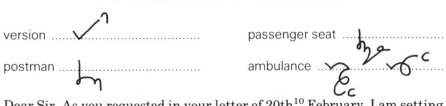

Dear Sir, As you requested in your letter of 20th[10] February, I am setting down here my account of the[20] accident that happened outside my house on New Year's Day.[30] You will appreciate that it is now almost two months[40] since the accident occurred, so it is possible that my[50] version will not be accurate in every detail. However, I[60] shall do my best. At about seven-thirty a.m. I[70] was in my front porch picking up my milk bottles[80] when I heard the screeching of car brakes. I looked[90] up and saw a blue car crashing into the back[100] of a yellow van which was parked opposite my house[110] on the other side of the road. The car was[120] being driven by a woman and there was a man[130] in the passenger seat. A postman was delivering mail to[140] a house near the parked van. He shouted to me[150] to phone for an ambulance, which I did. Yours truly[160]

Section Six
180-word passages

1 A letter about a problem with a neighbour

next-door neighbour ....   overhanging ....

branches ....   depriving ....

no reply ....

Dear Mrs Roberts, Thank you for your letter dated 15th[10] September which was on my desk when I returned to[20] work yesterday after a business trip to France. I was[30] sorry to read that you are having a little problem[40] with your next-door neighbour, but I do not advise[50] taking legal action at this stage. As you are not[60] on speaking terms with him at the present time, I[70] suggest you write to him pointing out that his apple[80] trees are overhanging your garden to an unreasonable extent, that[90] falling apples are damaging your flower beds, and that the[100] overhanging branches are depriving your plants of both sunlight and[110] rain. You should also mention the fact that the washing[120] on your line catches on the branches and, in fact,[130] one of your net curtains has been torn because of[140] this. If you receive no reply to your letter within[150] a couple of weeks, please do not hesitate to contact[160] me again and I shall consider what further steps might[170] be appropriate in order to resolve this matter. Yours sincerely[180]

2 A letter about stolen cheque books and credit cards

credit ....   card ....

credit card ....   anxious ....

signature ....   accordingly ....

expenditure ....

Dear Customer, We are writing to tell you what to[10] do in the event of your cheque book or credit[20] card being stolen. We have recently received several telephone calls[30] from anxious customers to whom this has happened. They were[40] all uncertain of their position if the thief should gain[50] access to their bank accounts. As one of our customers,[60] you have entered into a contract with us for which[70] we will provide certain services. One of these services is[80] to pay the holder of any cheque which has been [90] properly signed by you. If we pay the holder of[100] a cheque with a forged signature, then we will have[110] broken part of our contract with you and will credit[120] your account accordingly. Before doing so, however, we would need[130] to be certain that you had taken reasonable care to[140] avoid the theft. If a thief steals your credit card[150] you will probably be held responsible for only the first[160] fifty pounds of expenditure, provided you notify the credit-card[170] company immediately you become aware of its loss. Yours faithfully[180]

3 A letter objecting to a proposed motorway

alongside ....   excessive ....

currently ....   petition ....

Prime Minister ....

Dear Sir, I am writing to you in your capacity[10] as our local Member of Parliament. If articles in the[20] local newspaper are to be believed, then it would seem[30] that it is now proposed to build a motorway alongside[40] the estate where I live. I feel most strongly that[50] this would be a very unwise move. Firstly, the majority[60] of families on the estate have young children, and great[70] anxiety would result regarding their safety. Secondly, as the motorway[80] would provide a direct link between this town and the[90] city of Manchester, the stream of traffic it would attract[100] would be excessive and constant. Consequently, a problem would arise[110] from the noise and vibration this would cause. I am[120] currently in the process of compiling a petition, which I[130] sincerely hope you will present to the Prime Minister on[140] behalf of the vast number of people who have signed[150] it. Within the next few days you should receive a[160] copy of the said petition, which has been signed by[170] more than three thousand, five hundred local residents. Yours faithfully[180]

4 A letter about house security

we were very sorry ....   burglary ....

upward ....   brochures ....

Dear Mr Brown, We were very sorry to hear of[10] the recent burglary of your home and the subsequent losses[20] incurred. In order that an official claim for insurance can[30] be made, one of our representatives will call to see[40] you at your home. The number of burglaries taking place[50] is increasing year by year and causes a great deal[60] of distress to those affected. In an attempt to curb[70] this upward trend, perhaps more care should be paid to[80] home security. With this aim in mind, our representative will[90] bring along a range of brochures giving advice and suggestions[100] as to the best way of achieving this. The answer[110] could well lie in having a burglar alarm fitted. There[120] are many alarms on the market, of varying types and[130] prices. Our brochures are intended to act as a guide[140] to help you work your way through the range on[150] offer. Our representative will also give his expert advice. Please[160] would you telephone our office so that a convenient time[170] can be arranged for him to visit you. Yours sincerely[180]

5 A letter about a secretarial course

application ....{.................   essential ....۹.S................

successful ....&...............   interview ....

Dear Miss Cooper, Thank you for your completed application form[10] to join the Private Secretary's Certificate Course at this college.[20] I should just like to remind you that this is[30] a full-time course which lasts for thirty-six weeks[40] from September to July. The college day is from nine[50] in the morning until five in the afternoon. A considerable[60] amount of private study is required and it is essential[70] that students are prepared to give their own time to[80] this if they wish to be successful in the examinations[90] at the end of the course. I shall be glad[100] if you will attend for interview on Monday, 20th August[110] at two o'clock. On arrival at the college, please go[120] to the reception desk directly opposite the entrance, from where[130] you will be directed to the appropriate room. The tutor[140] will be expecting you and the interview will take about[150] thirty minutes. If you have any queries the tutor will,[160] of course, be happy to answer them. Please bring this[170] letter, together with proof of your examination results. Yours sincerely[180]

6 A letter from a hotel about Winter-weekend Breaks

nationally .....ſ...................   disappointment ....

breakfast ....&...................   January ...).................

(June ....).....................)

Dear Mr Peters, We hope you enjoyed your stay with[10] us last year, and we are now writing to let[20] you know about our Winter-weekend Break holidays. We are[30] sure you will be interested in these, and the enclosed[40] brochure will give you full details. As you know, we[50] are situated in a beautiful part of the country and[60] these breaks are very popular. For this reason, we are[70] writing to all our past guests to give them the[80] chance of booking before we advertise nationally. We expect a[90] very high demand for these weekend holidays, so we would[100] suggest that you return the enclosed booking slip as soon[110] as possible to avoid disappointment. The package will include accommodation[120] for two nights with full English breakfast, two dinners, VAT[130] and service charge. The cost will be thirty pounds per[140] person for the two days. You can choose any two[150] nights from Friday to Sunday. We do hope you will[160] take advantage of this special offer and we look forward[170] to meeting you again in January or February. Yours sincerely[180]

7 Travelling on motorways

inevitably ....   suddenly ....

cones ....   brewed ....

I wonder if anyone enjoys travelling on motorways. I remember[10] saying after my first motorway journey that I never wanted[20] to use one again. I have had to relent, but[30] I must say I still do not enjoy motorways. Unless[40] one leaves home in the early hours of the morning,[50] delays inevitably occur on any journey. Sometimes there seems no[60] reason for traffic jams; they suddenly clear and nothing can[70] be seen which might have caused the hold-up. At[80] other times there is the grim sight of a battered[90] car or two. This does seem to ensure that people[100] drive carefully for the next few miles, until they forget[110] what they have just seen. Then there are the lines[120] of cones stretching as far as the eye can see,[130] with no obvious work going on alongside. I have often[140] brewed tea in our motor caravan whilst stationary in a[150] long line of traffic. On one occasion, the passengers in[160] a coach were amused when their driver, seeing me knitting,[170] asked me to make him a jumper while we waited.[180]

8 A letter from a building society

in your letter ....   old-established ....

thousands of people ....   mortgage ....

favourably ....

Dear Sir, As requested in your letter of 18th February,[10] we are enclosing a copy of our booklet entitled *Owning*[20] *Your Own Home.* We are an old-established building society,[30] and over the years have helped many thousands of people[40] to own their own homes. Our mortgage rates compare very[50] favourably with those of our competitors, and we are quite[60] prepared to take into account joint salaries of husband and[70] wife when calculating the amount of money we are prepared[80] to lend. Your house purchase can be made over a[90] period of twenty-five years, with repayments kept to an[100] amount easily affordable by you. As well as lending money,[110] we act as agents for house sales and we have[120] many local properties on our books at present. These range[130] from link houses for first-time buyers to detached houses[140] with large gardens in delightful settings. If you will let[150] us know what type of property you are seeking, we[160] shall be very glad to send you details of suitable[170] homes. We look forward to hearing from you. Yours faithfully[180]

9 A letter about keeping children occupied during school holidays

days of the week ....   supervised ....

qualified ....

Dear Parent, Now that the long summer holiday from school[10] is approaching, you will, no doubt, be wondering how to[20] help your child to fill his or her days. This[30] is always a difficult task but it is especially so[40] when it is raining and outside activities are restricted. Our[50] organization, the Village Parents' Society, began last year to work[60] on the problem of keeping children occupied, and we believe[70] you may be interested in our solution. The Society has[80] taken the lease of an old village hall in the[90] High Street, and on three days of the week we[100] provide supervised games and classes for children from the ages[110] of seven to fourteen. We have qualified staff teaching such[120] subjects as knitting, model-making, local history and gardening. For[130] the younger children we have a play house and a[140] sand pit under cover. If you are interested in becoming[150] a member of our society and allowing your child to[160] use its facilities, please contact me at the village hall[170] on any Monday or Wednesday morning. Yours faithfully, Acting Secretary[180]

10 A letter about car repairs

undertaken ....   foreman ....

(fireman ....)   vehicle ....

regrettable ....

Dear Mr Wood, Thank you for your letter of 4th[10] May concerning the repairs to your car, from which I[20] note that early June will be a convenient time for[30] the work to be undertaken. I have spoken to the[40] foreman and have arranged for your vehicle to be booked[50] in at nine-thirty a.m. on Wednesday, 8th June. The[60] work will be completed by Tuesday, 14th June when we[70] will make arrangements with our secretary to have the car[80] delivered to your office. I am indeed very sorry that[90] your vehicle was damaged while in our care, and can[100] assure you that an enquiry is being made in an[110] effort to discover who is responsible. I note also that[120] this accident means you will have problems with your forthcoming[130] business trip. If you would kindly let me know your[140] dates of travel, I will arrange for a member of[150] my staff to take you to the airport and meet[160] you on your return. Please let me have your comments.[170] I apologize again for this most regrettable accident. Yours sincerely[180]

Section Seven
200-word passages

1 Notes from a Board meeting

inflation .... *[shorthand]* ....   interest rate ....

profit margin .... *[shorthand]* ....   overcome .... *[shorthand]* ....

industrial action .... *[shorthand]* ....

The following points emerged at yesterday's meeting which was held[10] to enable the Board of Directors to discuss the effects[20] of inflation on company profits. Firstly, when customers were given[30] credit, the interest rate charged to them was at too[40] low a level. This meant that by the time the[50] balance owing was cleared, inflation, rising at the levels it[60] is today, had an adverse effect and in real terms[70] our profit margin was lower than it appeared on paper.[80] To ovecome this state of affairs, it was decided to[90] raise the interest rates charged for credit. Secondly, the workforce[100] is growing very unsettled because the inflation rate has risen[110] faster than its wages. The Board decided to arrange talks[120] with union members to discuss the possibility of a pay[130] rise. The Board hopes that in the light of steps[140] being taken to reach an agreed pay settlement, the workforce[150] will decide against taking industrial action. A date and time[160] has yet to be arranged for the proposed talks to[170] take place, but it is expected that they will be[180] held within the next few days. It is most important[190] that all employees realize that positive action is being taken.[200]

2 A letter about a job interview

accountant .... *[shorthand]* ....   aptitude .... *[shorthand]* ....

alternative .... *[shorthand]* ....   certificates .... *[shorthand]* ....

in the meantime .... *[shorthand]* ....

Dear Miss Wilson, We are in receipt of your letter[10] applying for the post of senior secretary to our chief[20] accountant. Briefly, the position calls for a person with excellent[30] shorthand and keyboarding skills, together with a knowledge of word[40] processing. An aptitude for figure work would also be an[50] advantage, as would the ability to work under pressure and[60] meet deadlines. Informal interviews are being held during the week,[70] commencing 5th August. An appointment has been arranged for you[80] to attend at two o'clock on the Tuesday afternoon of[90] that week. If you are unable to attend for any[100] reason, please would you telephone the personnel department to make[110] an alternative appointment. When you attend for the interview, please[120] bring with you copies of your certificates and two references,[130] one of which should be from your present, or last,[140] employer. We note from your letter of application that you[150] have only just moved to the area. To help you[160] find your way, a map of the district, showing the[170] best route to our office, is enclosed. In the meantime,[180] should you have any queries, please do not hesitate to[190] contact me. I look forward to meeting you. Yours sincerely[200]

3 A circular letter about dog kennels

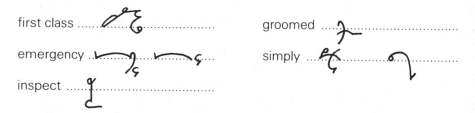

first class ....

emergency ....

inspect ....

groomed ....

simply ....

Dear Resident, The holiday season is nearly upon us again[10] and the problem arises of what to do with your[20] dog. We have the perfect solution for you. Why not[30] let your pet spend the time with us at our[40] first-class kennels? The kennels are of a very high[50] standard, with each animal having a kennel completely to itself.[60] Dogs are groomed on a daily basis by our well-[70]trained staff, who are all dog lovers. Every dog is[80] exercised twice each day, being taken for walks by our[90] staff in nearby parkland. While you are away there will[100] be no need for you to worry about the health[110] of your dog as we have our own resident vet.[120] The vet is on call twenty-four hours a day[130] should an emergency arise. If your pet has a liking[140] for certain types of food, this can be catered for.[150] Simply make a list of the preferred foods and hand[160] it to one of our staff; we will do the[170] rest. If you would like to inspect our kennels, feel[180] free to call in at any time, when one of[190] the staff will give you a conducted tour. Yours faithfully[200]

4 Composing a business letter

business letter .... clarify ....

paragraphs .... impression ....

If you work in an office, your boss may expect[10] you to compose some of his letters for him. Sometimes[20] he might dictate a few brief notes and leave you[30] to make them into a suitable letter. A business letter[40] can create a good or bad image of the firm,[50] so it is very important that you are able to[60] carry out this task in a competent way. First of[70] all, try to understand the purpose of the letter. If[80] you give it a heading, it will often help you[90] to clarify exactly what the main subject is. Next, plan[100] the letter very carefully. Arrange all the points in a[110] logical order and divide them into paragraphs. Pay special attention[120] to the first and last paragraphs. Do ensure that you[130] have achieved the right tone to suit the purpose of[140] the letter. Ask yourself how you would feel if you[150] received that letter and what your reaction would be. Finally,[160] make sure that the presentation of the letter is perfect.[170] The ideal letter will contain no spelling errors, be sensibly[180] punctuated, and be attractively displayed on the page. This kind[190] of letter will give a good impression of your company.[200]

5 The advantages and disadvantages of a centralized filing system

centralized .... throughout ....

economical .... thorough ....

disadvantages ....

A centralized filing system can have many advantages. One of[10] these is that a standard system of filing can be[20] used instead of having many different methods of filing throughout[30] one firm. The most suitable system can be developed and,[40] of course, all the equipment used can be the same.[50] This can be much more economical than having a variety[60] of systems. It is also possible to employ staff whose[70] only job is to maintain a good filing system. This[80] means that they will have a thorough training in the[90] work and will be more efficient than, say, a typist[100] who just files from time to time. There are, however,[110] disadvantages. Filing can sometimes be a rather dull task and[120] unless the staff are really interested in their job and[130] take a pride in what they are doing, they can[140] soon become bored with the work. Another drawback is that[150] it might not be possible to locate the central filing[160] area close to all the other departments. This could result[170] in time being wasted if files have to be collected[180] and returned. It may be that a mixture of central[190] and departmental filing is the best solution to the problem.[200]

6 A memo to a sales director

great care		exception	
discussion		(decision	)
amalgamating		costly	

I have looked with great care through the sales figures[10] for each of our areas over the past few years.[20] In each case the figures appear quite favourable, with one[30] exception. Our north-west area does not seem to be[40] doing well during this period, and I wonder whether you[50] can offer any explanation for this. I have asked our[60] area sales representative, John Brown, to come to Head Office[70] to see me on Tuesday next at 10.30 a.m.,[80] and I trust you will be able to join us[90] for a discussion. Will you please prepare a breakdown of[100] sales in the north-west area to bring with you.[110] I should like to see this split between large and[120] small customers, to see if it shows any trend. If[130] sales in the north-west continue to fall, we shall[140] have to give serious consideration to amalgamating north-west with[150] north-east to form a northern area, as it is[160] already proving too costly to keep a representative there with[170] such low sales. I do not think we should mention[180] this to John Brown on Tuesday. Your figures may show[190] a drop with one particular account on John Brown's books.[200]

7 An application for the position of personal assistant

edition		sales director	

Dear Sir, With reference to the advertisement in tonight's edition[10] of the *Evening Journal*, I should like to apply for[20] the position of personal assistant to the sales director. I[30] am thirty-five years old and have been a secretary[40] since leaving college. The jobs I have done have been[50] varied, and for several years I worked for the manager[60] of a very busy sales department where I had experience[70] of dealing with customers on the telephone, as well as[80] day-to-day contact with area sales representatives. It was[90] my responsibility to prepare the monthly sales figures for the[100] company, as well as providing a full secretarial service to[110] the manager. My qualifications exceed those stipulated in your advertisement,[120] as you will see from the copy of my c.v.[130] which is attached. You state that a word processor is[140] provided. I have had considerable experience with both computers and[150] word processors in my present post, and enjoy using them.[160] My present employer is aware that I am looking for[170] new employment, and is quite prepared to release me for[180] interview during office hours. If you require any further details,[190] I shall be pleased to furnish them immediately. Yours faithfully[200]

8 Mail-order shopping

mail order ....

conventional ....

period ....

outweigh ....

refrigerators ....

spread ....

exorbitant ....

Mail-order shopping has been a popular method of retailing[10] in the United Kingdom for many years, and it is[20] still expanding. Nowadays, armed with a big glossy catalogue, you[30] can order almost any items money can buy, from refrigerators[40] to records, from dresses to dressing tables. The choice of[50] supplier is also increasing yearly, with stylish High Street stores[60] joining the ranks of the established mail-order companies. If[70] you have little time or inclination to devote to conventional[80] shopping or you live a long way from a good[90] shopping centre, the mail-order company is a blessing. Should[100] you want a particular item, such as a pale pink[110] bathroom set, you may spend a day searching around town[120] when you could locate it in a few moments by[130] consulting the index of a mail-order catalogue. Mail order[140] also has the advantage of allowing you to spread your[150] payments over quite a long period of time, although it[160] should be noted that very high interest rates are often[170] involved in buying on credit and, where this is not[180] the case, the prices of the goods may well be[190] exorbitant. On the whole, however, the advantages outweigh the disadvantages.[200]

9 A letter requesting a reference

telephonist ....   switchboard ....

in addition ....   confidential ....

acknowledgement ....

Dear Mrs West, Miss Carol Black has applied to this[10] company for the post of clerk/typist and telephonist, and[20] has given your name as someone we may approach for[30] a reference on her behalf. The duties of the post[40] include providing a reception service for visitors to our offices[50] and operating the automatic telephone switchboard. In addition, the successful[60] applicant will have to offer a typing service to various[70] members of our sales staff and assist with the franking[80] of the mail. The hours of work will be from[90] eight-thirty a.m. to four-thirty p.m. with forty-five[100] minutes for lunch, but it may sometimes be necessary for[110] the person appointed to start work half an hour earlier[120] than usual to open and distribute the incoming mail. Updating[130] the company's notice board will also be a duty of[140] this post. I should be grateful to receive your comments[150] and confidential opinion of the suitability of Miss Black for[160] this post, and enclose a stamped addressed envelope for your[170] reply. In the interests of economy, an acknowledgement will not[180] be sent. May I take this opportunity of thanking you[190] for your assistance in this matter. Yours sincerely, Personnel Manager[200]

10 A letter offering employment

statutory ....   hours of work ....

eligible ....   Jennifer ....

Dear Miss Black, Following your interview yesterday, I have pleasure[10] in offering you the post of clerk/typist and telephonist[20] with this company. As discussed at the interview, your starting[30] salary will be six thousand, eight hundred pounds and you[40] will be entitled, during your first twelve months, to fourteen[50] days' holiday in addition to the statutory holidays. Your hours[60] of work will be eight-thirty a.m. to four-thirty[70] p.m. Monday to Friday with forty-five minutes for lunch[80] each day. Occasionally you may be asked to begin work[90] at 8 o'clock in order to assist with the incoming[100] mail. You will recall that at the interview we mentioned[110] we would like you to gain additional qualifications in typewriting,[120] and we have therefore arranged that in September you will[130] begin a day-release course at the local technical college[140] where you will study typewriting, office practice, word processing and[150] English. This course will continue until June next year and,[160] if you obtain passes in these subjects, you will be[170] eligible for a two-hundred pound increase in salary. Please[180] report to Mrs Jennifer Jones in the personnel department at[190] nine a.m. on Monday, 8th August. Yours sincerely, Personnel Manager[200]

Section Eight
220-word passages

1 A letter about a poor central-heating maintenance service

supposedly

priority

noisier

managing director

deplorable

Dear Sir, I am writing as a very disappointed customer[10] to complain of the service I have received from your[20] company. I pay an annual maintenance charge for my central-[30]heating system and I am supposedly guaranteed a forty-eight[40] hour service and priority treatment. I rang your office last[50] Monday at ten a.m. to report that my heating system[60] had failed. After three more telephone calls, an engineer was[70] eventually sent on Thursday afternoon to repair the system. He[80] could not effect a repair then because he did not[90] have the parts, but came back on Friday morning to[100] complete the job. He spent most of Friday morning at[110] my house and almost one hour of that time was[120] spent on my telephone, at my expense, seeking advice from[130] another engineer. The system was eventually switched back on at[140] noon on Friday. The system was noisier than previously, but[150] I was assured that it was all right. It is[160] now Saturday morning and the system has failed again. I[170] have telephoned your office and talked to an answering machine,[180] but I have also decided to write to you, as[190] the company managing director, in the hope that you will[200] ensure that steps are taken to improve what I can[210] only describe as a deplorable service to customers. Yours faithfully[220]

2 A reply to an enquiry about off-peak holidays

literature

exotic

off-peak

freephone

pro-forma

Dear Mr Brown, Thank you for your recent enquiry about[10] our range of holidays. I am pleased to enclose the[20] selection of brochures you requested. You will see from just[30] a quick study of the literature that we have a[40] huge range of holidays available. We cover everything from coach[50] tours in Britain and Europe to flights on Concorde and[60] holidays in the most exotic places. We think that because[70] we use excellent hotels, and offer holidays outside the traditional[80] peak periods, we give especially good value for money. An[90] advantage of holidays at off-peak times is that you[100] avoid the worst crowds and delays, and you also receive[110] an even better standard of service and attention from your[120] hotel staff. We are able to offer attractive coach or[130] rail options so you may choose the best travel arrangements[140] for you to reach your holiday destination in comfort. With[150] our company you can book by telephone on a free[160] line from the comfort of your own home. You talk[170] to the very people who will arrange your holiday. We[180] are pleased to offer our freephone reservation service but, if[190] you prefer to book your holiday by post, you may[200] use the easily completed pro-forma and return it in[210] the pre-paid envelope enclosed with our literature. Yours sincerely[220]

3 Starting your own business

shortage .... self-employed ....

bookkeeper .... necessity ....

encounter ....

Owing to the shortage of jobs available today, many people[10] are considering the possibility of becoming self-employed. There is[20] a great deal more responsibility attached to being self-employed[30] than in being an employee. In the first place, much[40] self-discipline is required. When the sun is shining and[50] there is nobody to give you orders, it can be[60] very difficult to make yourself work. Another point to bear[70] in mind is that you need to become master of[80] many trades. You may, for example, have to act as[90] a buyer, a salesperson and a bookkeeper. It can be[100] very trying when, at the end of a hard day's[110] work, you must sit down at a desk or table[120] and deal with the necessary paperwork. The full support of[130] your family is also a necessity to help you through[140] the early and most difficult days of establishing your business.[150] The support of your bank manager is highly desirable, as[160] he can help you with the financial side of the[170] business. It will be his help you will need if,[180] for instance, you encounter a cash-flow problem. However, the[190] rewards of running your own business can far outweigh the[200] worries. There is much satisfaction to be gained from starting[210] a project entirely on your own and making it grow.[220]

4 Sensible dieting

manufacturers ....   dieting ....

(dating ....)   orange ....

permanent ....

Dieting is big business. Millions of pounds every year are[10] made by the manufacturers of dieting aids. It is difficult[20] to understand why so many people are tricked into buying[30] these so-called miracle slimming aids when medical experts tell[40] us that to lose weight we must simply reduce our[50] intake of food. Of course, weight is lost more quickly[60] if certain kinds of food are given up completely: for[70] instance, cakes and the ever-popular chips which soak up[80] the oil or fat in which they are fried. However,[90] the kind of 'crash diet', where you literally starve yourself[100] for a few days in the hope of shedding a[110] few pounds, should be avoided at all costs. Such diets[120] are bad for your health and the weight lost just[130] creeps back on again when a normal eating pattern is[140] resumed. The best solution is to alter your eating habits[150] permanently. Remove from your diet foods which have a high[160] fat content and those which contain an excess of sugar.[180] Eat plenty of fresh fruit and vegetables. When you feel[190] like a snack, eat an apple or an orange instead[200] of a chocolate bar. By altering your diet on a[210] permanent basis, the weight you lose should not be regained.[220]

5 A letter about redundancies

unanimously ....   redundant ....

circular ....   voluntary ....

approximately ....

Dear Mr Walton, Further to the meeting of the Board[10] of Directors last week, it is, regrettably, my task to[20] inform you of the outcome. The Board decided, unanimously, to[30] make drastic cuts in the number of our employees. In[40] effect, this means there will be job losses totalling one[50] hundred and fifty-five. In your capacity as works manager,[60] it falls to you to submit a list of the[70] employees who will be made redundant. When compiling this list,[80] the policy should be first to explain the situation, by[90] means of a circular letter, to the entire workforce. In[100] this letter, make it known that those wishing to apply[110] for voluntary redundancy will be granted this. The next step[120] will be to determine those employees who have spent the[130] least time with the company, in other words, use the[140] established principle of 'last in, first out'. The Board would,[150] of course, have liked to dispose of some jobs through[160] natural wastage. However, as the cuts must come into effect[170] immediately, it is not possible to do so. It will[180] be necessary for you to attend the next Board meeting[190] to be held in approximately ten days' time, and submit[200] the redundancy list. The Board regrets taking this action, but[210] in the present circumstances there is no alternative. Yours faithfully[220]

6 A letter confirming a hotel reservation

reservation ...~~~~~~~~~~~~~~~~~~~   husband ...~~~~~~~~~~~~~~~~~~~

late ...~~~~~~~~~~~~~~~~~~~   light ...~~~~~~~~~~~~~~~~~~~

Dear Sirs, With reference to our telephone conversation of this[10] morning, I am writing to confirm my reservation. As I[20] told you, I shall require one double room with bathroom[30] for myself and my husband, and one single room with[40] bathroom for my son, aged fourteen. We shall be arriving[50] at the hotel on Friday, 10th August and leaving after[60] breakfast on Sunday, 12th August. As it is not possible[70] to leave here until my husband finishes work on the[80] Friday, we shall probably not be able to get to[90] the hotel until nine or ten at night. We realize[100] that this is too late for dinner, but we should[110] be grateful if you could provide us with a light[120] meal when we arrive. We would be quite happy to[130] have this on a tray in our room if this[140] is easier for you to arrange. We shall require breakfast[150] on the Saturday and Sunday mornings and dinner on Saturday[160] evening. As I mentioned to you on the telephone, we[170] would prefer to have rooms facing the sea if this[180] is possible. As you requested, I am enclosing my cheque[190] for thirty pounds as deposit, and look forward to receiving[200] your confirmation of my booking. Could you also send me[210] a map showing the location of the hotel? Yours faithfully[220]

7 A letter about a development of luxury houses and bungalows

thank you for your enquiry ....   development ....

luxury ....   railway station ....

bungalows ....

Dear Madam, Thank you for your enquiry about our new[10] development of luxury homes. These are being built on the[20] edge of the town, and are within walking distance of[30] shops and schools. There is a good bus service into[40] the centre of town and the main line railway station[50] is ten minutes' drive away, with a good train service[60] to London. There will be twenty houses and bungalows, some[70] with four bedrooms and some with three. All the properties[80] will have a sitting room and separate dining room. They[90] will have two bathrooms, and a large kitchen which will[100] be fitted with a cooker and dishwasher. The enclosed plans[110] show the designs of the different types of houses and[120] bungalows and also give room measurements. Outside there will be[130] a double garage with large drive and paths all around[140] the house. The front and rear gardens will be levelled[150] and sown with grass. The building is being carried out[160] by a well-known firm of local builders who have[170] a very good reputation in this district. All the materials[180] used are of the best quality. A site plan is[190] also enclosed showing the exact location of the properties. The[200] show house is open to the public on Saturdays and[210] Sundays and at all other times by appointment. Yours faithfully[220]

8 A letter requesting conference accommodation

Friday evening ....   ante-room ....

Saturday evening ....   photocopier ....

provisional ....

Dear Sir, I am writing to enquire whether you are[10] able to accommodate the annual conference of our society, which[20] is to be held in Bath in two years' time.[30] It will be during the Easter vacation and we anticipate[40] an attendance of two hundred over one weekend, from Friday[50] evening to tea-time on Sunday. We shall require a[60] buffet supper on the Friday evening, then full meals through[70] to Sunday lunch. We should like coffee and tea to[80] be served in an ante-room to the conference hall[90] at mid-morning and mid-afternoon breaks, to keep these[100] to a minimum. Breakfast and lunch could be self-service,[110] but we wish to hold a formal dinner on the[120] Saturday evening. As well as the main conference hall, we[130] shall require two smaller meeting rooms for both Friday and[140] Saturday evenings from about nine o'clock. We shall require secretarial[150] services, including the use of a photocopier. It is also[160] important that there are adequate telephones for newspaper reporters to[170] use. We assume you have slide-projection facilities in the[180] lecture theatre you would allocate for our conference. If you[190] are interested in accommodating us, I should be glad to[200] hear from you as soon as possible. A provisional quotation[210] and some sample menus would be much appreciated. Yours faithfully[220]

9 Open learning

inception ....   programmes ....

indexing ....   encouragement ....

tremendously ....

Many opportunities now exist for studying at home. This appeals[10] to those who live a long way from a town,[20] or who do shift work, or cannot leave the house[30] on a regular basis, or are handicapped. Everyone will have[40] heard of the Open University, which has attracted many thousands[50] of students since its inception. Even if not studying one[60] of its courses, it is interesting to listen to the[70] radio programmes which accompany its study material. These are late[80] at night, but worth staying up for if you find[90] the subject-matter interesting. Open College is a recent development,[100] and is for less academic courses than those offered by[110] the Open University. Local colleges of further education will be[120] pleased to provide details. Such establishments have offered open learning[130] for several years and have found that, in general, it[140] works well. Most subjects are offered, and there is a[150] national indexing system so that would-be students can find[160] out who runs the courses they require. Apart from attending[170] tutorials, the students can keep in touch with their tutors[180] by letter or telephone during the progress of the course.[190] Tutors find that many open-learning students need a lot[200] of encouragement, and if they can be put in touch[210] with students doing the same course it helps them tremendously.[220]

10 A letter giving particulars of a house for sale

Baxter .... suitable ....

stable ....

Dear Mr and Mrs Baxter, Thank you for your letter[10] dated 11th September, in which you describe the type of[20] property you wish to purchase. We are pleased to enclose[30] particulars of two properties currently on our books which we[40] think will be of interest to you. Both properties are[50] detached houses in their own grounds, with central heating and[60] double garages, and are within your price range of seventy[70] to ninety thousand pounds; although only one of them is[80] situated in the area you particularly favour. I give below[90] some details of the more suitable property called Oak Cottage.[100] This is a three-storey building with three double and[110] four single bedrooms. It also has a study on the[120] second floor, and three large reception rooms together with a[130] newly fitted kitchen on the ground floor. The property stands[140] in three acres of land and there is a small[150] lake at the front of the house. In the grounds[160] at the rear are a stable block and a garage[170] for two vehicles. We recommend that you make an appointment[180] to view Oak Cottage as we feel sure you will[190] find that it meets your requirements. With an asking price[200] of eighty-four thousand pounds, it is well within your[210] price range. Please telephone for an early appointment. Yours sincerely[220]

Section Nine
240-word passages

1 A letter about an overdrawn bank account

escaped ....   debit balance ....

schemes ....   unexpected ....

Dear Madam, It can hardly have escaped your notice that[10] your account with this bank is once again overdrawn. On[20] this occasion, the debit balance is exactly two hundred and[30] forty-four pounds. You will appreciate that we cannot possibly[40] allow this situation to continue, and I should therefore be[50] much obliged if you would telephone my secretary at your[60] earliest convenience in order that she can arrange for you[70] to call in and discuss the matter with me. I[80] must point out that you have placed yourself in a[90] similar position no fewer than three times in the past[100] two years, and I feel we would both benefit from[110] a thorough review of your financial affairs. It may be[120] that the bank can be of assistance to you by[130] arranging proper overdraft facilities or a personal loan. We have[140] a number of schemes which are designed to help customers[150] who suddenly find themselves in need of a little extra[160] cash or even a considerable sum to pay an unexpected[170] bill. I shall explain these schemes at our meeting. In[180] the meantime, I have to inform you that interest at[190] the appropriate rate will be charged on the two hundred[200] and forty-four pounds which you have borrowed from us[210] without permission and, of course, we shall not allow any[220] more payments to be made from your account. I look[230] forward to seeing you in the near future. Yours faithfully[240]

2 A proposed barrage across a river

precious ....   standard of living ....

livelihood ....   environment ....

No doubt those of you who receive the local evening[10] newspaper will have read some of the many articles which[20] have appeared in it over the last few months concerning[30] the proposed barrage across the river. What many people do[40] not realize is the effect this will have on farmers[50] in the area. Once the barrage is completed, thousands of[60] acres of grazing land will be flooded to provide a[70] suitable habitat for water fowl and other wildlife. Much precious[80] land will be taken from farmers whose families have made[90] their living for centuries working on the land. Many of[100] them will lose more than half their grazing pasture. This[110] means that they will have to sell their family homes[120] and move to another area in order to provide them[130] with the opportunity to maintain the standard of living to[140] which they have become accustomed. Who are these planners who[150] have given no thought to the families who will lose[160] their livelihood for the sake of a few birds? How[170] would they like to be forced from their homes because[180] it is thought that birds are more important and need[190] a better environment? I am in favour of protecting nature,[200] but not if doing so means the destruction of people's[210] homes and farming land. There are vast areas of waste[220] land in this district which are of little use for[230] farming, but would provide an ideal location for water fowl.[240]

3 The value of good service and customer relations

plumber ....

windscreen ....

old-fashioned ....

reluctant ....

We all know the difference between good service and bad[10] service when we are customers at the receiving end. The[20] plumber who does a first-class job at short notice[30] in your home and then clears up the mess afterwards[40] is giving you a good service. You will not quickly[50] forget the petrol station where your tank is filled up[60] for you, and your windscreen washed and polished at the[70] same time! This type of old-fashioned service makes a[80] big impression on customers, who are much more likely to[90] return with follow-up business in future and to tell[100] their friends. Several surveys have shown that services to customers[110] are better now than they were a few years ago[120] and, of course, at a time when business activity is[130] becoming more and more competitive, good customer service is essential[140] if a company is to be successful. There are still[150] some people who are reluctant to complain if they are[160] dissatisfied. But this situation is changing as consumers become better[170] educated and informed. Not many of us like to make[180] a scene, but these unpleasant situations may often be avoided[190] if we take the trouble to deal only with companies[200] of good repute. Probably the best insurance against poor service[210] is to heed the personal warnings and recommendations of family[220] and friends. Personal recommendation is also the very best form[230] of advertising for a company that gives an excellent service.[240]

4 A memo about photocopying costs

photocopying ⟨shorthand⟩ ⟨shorthand⟩   electronic ⟨shorthand⟩

infringe ⟨shorthand⟩   co-operation ⟨shorthand⟩

The accounts department has just issued figures for departmental expenditure[10] which show that photocopying costs have exceeded the budgeted cost[20] several times over. Possibly the budget was set too low,[30] and uses for photocopying have now been found that were[40] not expected. Use of the machine will be reviewed and[50] the budget adjusted accordingly. However, it is desirable that departments[60] making use of the photocopying facility should bear the cost[70] in proportion to the amount of use to which they[80] put the facility. For this reason, the present free access[90] to the machine will in future be more closely controlled.[100] Each departmental head will be provided with an electronic key[110] which must be inserted into the machine for it to[120] function. The key incorporates a counter so that each department[130] will be able to monitor its own use of the[140] copier by reference to its departmental count and be charged[150] accordingly. A key will be available from the clerk in[160] the personnel department for employees who wish to copy personal[170] material for their own private use. This key may be[180] used provided that the employee does not infringe any copyright[190] on the material copied, that a charge of three pence[200] per copy is paid to cover copying costs, and that[210] the number of copies made by any employee does not[220] exceed ten per week. The co-operation of all staff members[230] is requested to ensure the success of these new procedures.[240]

5 A letter to Mrs Brown about repairs to her car

first thing in the morning ⟨shorthand⟩   second-hand ⟨shorthand⟩

Dear Mrs Brown, We are pleased to inform you that[10] we have now obtained the parts we require to repair[20] your car. We should therefore be grateful if you could[30] telephone us as soon as possible to arrange a date[40] for us to have the car in our workshop. As[50] we explained to you when we discussed the problem with[60] your car, it is advisable for this repair work to[70] be carried out without delay, because if you continue to[80] drive the car in this condition you may cause further[90] damage to the engine. It will be necessary for us[100] to work on the car for a complete day and[110] we should need to start first thing in the morning.[120] We would be happy to drive you back home after[130] you have brought the car to us and we could[140] probably deliver it to your home at the end of[150] the day, if this would be helpful to you. Alternatively,[160] if you need transport during the day we could arrange[170] for you to hire one of our cars at a[180] special price of ten pounds. Whilst writing to you, we[190] should like to draw your attention to the fact that[200] we have now opened our new showrooms. These provide a[210] suitable setting for our display of new and second-hand[220] cars, and include a comfortable waiting room for our customers.[230] We look forward to hearing from you. Yours sincerely, Manager[240]

6 Some advice on taking telephone messages

it is likely		omit	
great importance		extension	

If you have to answer the telephone at work, it[10] is likely that you will sometimes have to take a[20] message for someone who is not there. It is absolutely[30] vital that you write down all the details, and that[40] you make sure that the message is received by the[50] person concerned when they return. It is very tempting to[60] think that you will remember everything that has been said,[70] and if you are busy you may think you will[80] save time by not stopping to write it all down.[90] This is a mistake. By the time you see the[100] person, many things will have happened in the meantime and[110] your mind will be full of other matters. It is[120] so easy to forget part of the message and perhaps[130] omit something that was of great importance. The first thing[140] to ask is the name of the caller. Do not[150] be afraid to ask them to spell this out for[160] you if you are not sure you have got it[170] right. You will also need to know their telephone number,[180] and their extension, if they have one. Next, write down[190] very clear details of the message they want to leave,[200] and make a note as to whether they want the[210] call returned. Finally, mark it clearly with the name of[220] the person they asked for, put the date and time[230] on it, and sign it. Printed forms are very useful.[240]

7 A letter about printing a programme

association		obviously	
emblem		art-work	

Dear Sirs, My association would greatly appreciate your advice on[10] the production of our programme. We issue this twice yearly[20] and need approximately three hundred copies each time. Until now[30] we have duplicated the programme ourselves on an ink duplicator,[40] but at our last annual general meeting it was recommended[50] that a better-quality programme should be produced. We therefore[60] have in mind a thin coloured card. This would have[70] to be printed on both sides and folded in some[80] way. We think it might well be best to use[90] A4 size and fold it into three, as this would[100] just about fit into a wallet or pocket. Our emblem[110] would appear on the front cover, but all the rest[120] would be typewritten. It will probably need to be reduced[130] once it is typed, in order to fit on to[140] the required size. We do have facilities for reducing on[150] a photocopier. We should be glad to have some guidance[160] from you on the type of ribbon which would reproduce[170] best. Would this be a carbon ribbon? Obviously the photocopy[180] would need to be good in order to reproduce well.[190] Should we stick the emblem in place with paste and[200] photocopy this at the same time? If we did all[210] the art-work ourselves, would it cut down the cost[220] of printing? Please let us know what colour card you[230] can offer. A sample would be appreciated. Yours faithfully, Secretary[240]

8 A letter about exchange visits for students

exchange ....   bus service ....

in the past ....   member of staff ....

Dear Parent, I am writing to give you full details[10] of the exchange visits planned for this summer, so that[20] you may decide whether you wish your son or daughter[30] to take part. Our students will be visiting Germany for[40] two weeks commencing 20th June, and the cost will be[50] ninety-five pounds. This will include everything except spending money,[60] and it is recommended that you limit the latter to[70] forty-five pounds. Accommodation will be in the homes of[80] the German students, and there will be very little expenditure[90] on fares whilst the students are attending college in Germany,[100] as a private bus service is provided. Travel will be[110] by train and ferry. We have in the past used[120] a coach but, as we have obtained very good bargain[130] prices from German Railways, this year it has been decided[140] to go by train. There will be reserved seats all[150] the way through. We shall use a night ferry so[160] that students can sleep on the boat. There will be[170] one member of staff to every eight students. The German[180] students will be coming for the two weeks commencing 14th[190] July. They will, of course, be accommodated in the homes[200] of our students, so it is important that you have[210] a spare room to offer. If you are interested in[220] sending your son or daughter on this exchange, please complete[230] the form below and return it to me. Yours sincerely[240]

9 A letter about moving house

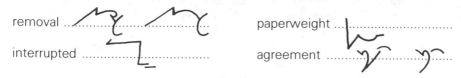

removal .... paperweight ....

interrupted .... agreement ....

Dear Jane, I was delighted to receive your letter and[10] to hear that you will be moving to Somerset next[20] month. I know that this is the first time you[30] have moved home and am pleased to give you some[40] advice. As you know, Paul and I moved here six[50] months ago, but the day did not go well. If[60] I tell you about the problems we had, you will[70] probably benefit from our experience. Firstly, the removal men did[80] not arrive until ten-thirty which meant we were unable[90] to hand over our keys to the purchasers until later[100] than agreed. Then the removal men damaged our antique book[110] case by dropping a heavy paperweight on it. The second[120] removal van was late. When it arrived work was resumed,[130] although frequently interrupted by breaks for cups of tea or[140] coffee. When we finally reached our new home, sixty miles[150] away, we found only one removal van was there. It[160] was another hour before the second van arrived because the[170] driver had got lost! There were other disasters: for instance,[180] two china plates were broken and we have not yet[190] found the kitchen clock! Although these events were upsetting, we[200] were covered by the agreement made with the removal firm[210] and our claim has now been settled. I advise you[220] to check carefully the agreement you make with your removers,[230] and hope you have a trouble-free day. Regards, Christine[240]

10 A letter following a parish council meeting

quarterly .... investigate ....

donation .... treasurer ....

Dear Mr Wells, Following the quarterly meeting of the Parish[10] Council held on Friday, at which you were unable to[20] be present, I have been asked to draw your attention[30] to the following matters arising. It was felt by the[40] members that the account for one hundred and forty pounds,[50] representing the quarterly telephone bill, was excessive. You are therefore[60] requested to investigate this matter and report to the next[70] meeting to be held in July. On a more cheerful[80] note, the committee wish me to extend their thanks to[90] you for the hard work you undertook recently when planning[100] the May Day celebrations. The event was well organized and[110] raised a lot of money for the village. Everyone seemed[120] to enjoy themselves and the Council has had a number[130] of letters praising the competition for the May Queen, and[140] the crowning ceremony on the village green. Some of the[150] money raised has enabled us to make a donation of[160] two hundred pounds to the church for repairs to the[170] spire. As you may already know, our treasurer, Mr Williams,[180] is leaving the area and as a result must resign[190] his position on our committee. I have been asked by[200] our chairman to approach you to offer you this post.[210] It is our hope that you will accept this position[220] of responsibility, and I look forward to hearing from you[230] so that we may put this into effect. Yours sincerely[240]

Section Ten
260-word passages

1 Natural beauty products

hundreds of ....*e*...............   chemicals ....

ingredients ....*[shorthand]*.......   comprehensive ....

thousands of years ago ....*[shorthand]*.......

It is a very common thing these days to be[10] not only concerned about the amount of exercise we take[20] but also about our diet. Healthy living is no longer[30] a short-lived practice. You only have to look at[40] the hundreds of shoppers examining the contents of labels on[50] tins and packets in an endeavour to avoid consuming all[60] those dreaded additives to realize this. It is a great[70] shame that people do not take as much care about[80] the chemicals in other products which they use. Have you[90] ever seen a bottle of shampoo or a bar of[100] soap with a list of ingredients? If you want a[110] firm guarantee that the items you use are free from[120] harmful chemicals and, even better, not tested on animals, then[130] there are many items available to you. A new chain[140] of shops called 'Nature's Way' is opening all over the[150] country. If you care about animals and also about what[160] you put on your skin, then these are the shops[170] for you. A comprehensive range of products for hair, skin[180] and beauty treatments are produced from natural extracts from herbs[190] and flowers. These extracts were used thousands of years ago[200] by our ancestors. Today, few people can be bothered to[210] go and look for them so they are now bottled[220] and packed and made available at little cost. A range[230] of cosmetics are available with no lanolin added and none[240] is tested on animals. If you care about what you[250] eat, why not start caring about other products you use?[260]

2 A letter from a manufacturing jeweller

repairer ....*[shorthand]*...............   semi-precious ....*[shorthand]*.......

towards the ....*[shorthand]*...............

Dear Sir, I was interested to read in the April[10] issue of the *Jewellers' Guide to Precious Stones* that your[20] company has devised a new method of stone setting. As[30] a manufacturing jeweller and repairer, I am anxious to find[40] out more about this new method which, you claim, has[50] none of the drawbacks of the traditional claw-setting method.[60] Over the years my staff and I have experimented with[70] different ways of setting both precious and semi-precious stones,[80] but we have failed to discover any way that is[90] entirely free from problems. We should, therefore, be most interested[100] to learn more about your method. Towards the end of[110] your article you state that courses are available on your[120] premises for groups of between four and six people. At[130] present, I employ twelve full-time setters and several part-[140]timers, all of whom I would be willing to release[150] for one or two days a week to receive instruction[160] from you. Perhaps you would be good enough to let[170] me have full particulars of course fees including any discounts[180] you may be able to offer. If we can reach[190] agreement on the fees, I would want my staff to[200] attend the first available course in the New Year. In[210] that event, I shall need to make alterations to our[220] work schedules, and it would therefore be greatly appreciated if[230] you could reply to this letter as soon as possible.[240] Should you wish to contact me by telephone, please make[250] your call any day before noon. Yours faithfully, Barry Harper[260]

3 A sales letter about holidays

glorious ....

self-catering ....

action-packed ....

discounted ....

Dear Client, At the present time, we are offering large[10] discounts on selected package holidays, both in this country and[20] abroad. The holidays which qualify for this discount are many[30] and varied, catering for all tastes. Perhaps we could tempt[40] you with two weeks in the glorious Spanish sunshine, relaxing[50] on the soft sand of the beautiful beaches. Spain caters[60] for those who enjoy action-packed days and a lively[70] nightlife, but it also has plenty to offer those who[80] enjoy a more serene and 'away from it all' type[90] of holiday. Away from the crowded tourist spots on the[100] coast, delightful little villages can be found. Sample the real[110] Spain by spending time in these villages. Watch the farming[120] community at work, picking oranges, lemons and peaches. For those[130] who prefer to spend their holidays in Britain, we have[140] packages available in seaside resorts, the countryside and the big[150] cities. Holidays can be booked on a self-catering, half-[160]board or full-board basis. Conducted tours of interesting areas[170] are operated throughout the destinations on offer. These tours are[180] not included in the package price but will be charged[190] for separately at very modest rates. The discounts available are,[200] in some cases, as high as forty per cent. This[210] offer will not be advertised to the general public: it[220] is reserved for valued clients such as yourself. The discounted[230] packages will be offered on a first-come-first-served[240] basis, so if you are interested please do not delay[250] in contacting our booking office for full details. Yours faithfully[260]

4 Tourist information offices

well stocked .... *Ϟ̲ɕ* ....   theatre .... *⌐* ....

There are tourist information offices in many towns and cities.[10] They can also be found on some main roads where[20] a caravan has been made into an office and parked[30] at a convenient stopping place. The staff are specially trained,[40] and are able to give help and advice on all[50] kinds of local matters. The offices are also well stocked[60] with leaflets, guides and maps, which you can take away[70] and read at your leisure. You will find information on[80] all the local beauty spots and buildings of interest. There[90] will also be details of special events, such as art[100] exhibitions and concerts. The staff can probably tell you about[110] bus and train services, and even whether there are any[120] major roadworks in the area which might cause delays. It[130] is often not realized that these offices also have lists[140] of accommodation so, if you have arrived somewhere without booking[150] in advance, it is worth asking about hotels, inns and[160] guest houses. Many of these information centres are able to[170] make a booking for you, although they may charge for[180] the phone call. Some can even book theatre tickets for[190] you. Even if you are not a tourist, you may[200] find it interesting to visit the office in your area[210] to have a look at the leaflets and see what[220] is happening in your district. You may discover some new[230] places of interest that you did not know about. Whether[240] you are a tourist or a local resident, you will[250] certainly find the staff friendly and willing to help you.[260]

5 A notice about the arrangements for moving to new office premises

premises ...... *↑ϟ* ....   no point .... *ꝑ* .... *ꝏ.* ....
promptly ...... *↑⌐* ....

The date of the move to our new office premises[10] is now exactly six months away. Whilst this may seem[20] a very long way ahead, I assure you that the[30] time will pass all too quickly, and this notice is[40] to remind you of the plans we have made and[50] of the work that has to be done in the[60] meantime. I should like each department to start checking through[70] its filing system now. If there is anything out of[80] date and no longer needed, please throw it away. There[90] is no point in taking a large amount of paperwork[100] with us if it is not really needed. You will[110] see from the attached plan that each item of equipment[120] has been given a number. Will you please make sure[130] that this number, together with the number of the new[140] room, is displayed very clearly on all your equipment. This[150] will ensure that everything can be put in its correct[160] place by the delivery men on the day of the[170] move. During the next few weeks we are planning to[180] take all staff to see the new premises. Bring the[190] plan with you and if you have any suggestions to[200] make which you feel will improve the layout of the[210] offices, please let me know. We must try to get[220] everything right before we move so that we do not[230] have to make too many changes once we are installed.[240] Please remember that staff are expected to assist on Saturday,[250] 4th June, so that work can commence promptly on Monday.[260]

6 Working at home

merchandise .... (merchants ....)

predominate ....   theses ....

manuscripts ....

If you are unable to find a job, or if[10] you have decided to retire early but are still fairly[20] active, you may be looking for some sort of job[30] to do at home. A glance through the local paper[40] may well show you what opportunities exist in your area.[50] You might see advertisements for telephone sales personnel, who must[60] have a permanent address and, of course, a telephone. There[70] is a vast range of merchandise sold over the telephone,[80] but fitted kitchens and double-glazing seem to predominate. If[90] you can see yourself in the role of a salesperson,[100] then this could be the opening for you. If, however,[110] you prefer something more practical, there is assembly work to[120] consider. You will need to be good with your hands[130] to do this, and firms often prefer women because they[140] usually have smaller and more supple fingers than men. Sometimes[150] work is delivered to your home, but sometimes it is[160] up to you to collect and return it. A minimum[170] quantity per week may be stipulated, and you will need[180] to decide whether you can cope with this amount. Another[190] point worth bearing in mind, is that assembling the same[200] component time after time could soon become boring. If you[210] type you may find a ready market for your services.[220] A newspaper advertisement may be all that is required to[230] get you off the ground. Offer to type theses, reports,[240] manuscripts or business documents. If you produce good-quality work,[250] the demand for your services should increase as time passes.[260]

7 A letter about an insurance claim

whirlwind ....

handrail ....

ramp ....

assessor ....

greenhouse ....

Dear Sirs, I was disturbed to note from your letter[10] dated 26th March that you are not willing to pay[20] for the renewal of the railings to my front steps,[30] which were torn out by the whirlwind we experienced recently.[40] You refer to this handrail as a fence, and state[50] that fences are not covered by insurance. My dictionary defines[60] a fence as a boundary structure between adjoining properties or[70] parts of a property. The handrail to my front steps[80] is in no way a boundary structure; it is there[90] to prevent people from falling on to the road as[100] they go in or out of the front door. There[110] are five steps one side and a ramp on the[120] other side. It is quite dangerous without a handrail because[130] if a visitor knocked at the door and then took[140] a couple of steps backwards, he or she could fall[150] several feet on to the road. I have had to[160] provide a temporary rail in order to prevent this. It[170] seems to me that you have not read the builder's[180] estimate correctly, and if you look again you will see[190] it states 'post and rail'. You have assumed this to[200] be a division between my property and my neighbour's. Will[210] you please look into this matter again and, if necessary,[220] send an assessor to see for himself? I note that[230] you are prepared to cover the damage which occurred to[240] the greenhouse glass and to the two flower tubs, and[250] I look forward to receiving your cheque shortly. Yours faithfully[260]

8 An office memo

catalogue number ....

delivery date ....

urgent ....

reflection ....

personally ....

Monday morning ....

Memo to sales department manager: It has been brought to[10] my attention that an order placed by our customers Collins[20] and Brown has not been despatched, although when we accepted[30] the order it was agreed that the goods would be[40] delivered by last Monday. Their order, number eight five one,[50] was for two hundred pairs of size ten blue jeans,[60] catalogue number A-four five; fifty pairs of size fourteen[70] grey jeans, catalogue number A-four seven; and fifty size[80] ten blue cotton skirts, catalogue number A-four nine. The[90] company received our advice note, numbered six seven two, on[100] 11th July, stating that the goods would be despatched in[110] time to meet the agreed delivery date. This is a[120] most serious matter, and I wish you to make urgent[130] enquiries and report to me by the end of today,[140] explaining why the goods have not been delivered. It is[150] important that there is no repetition of this with any[160] company as it is a poor reflection on the standard[170] of our work and the reliability of our word. Please[180] also arrange to allow Collins and Brown a five per[190] cent discount when the account is due to be settled.[200] Let me have a copy of the memo to this[210] effect that you send to the accounts department, and I[220] will write personally to the company apologizing and explaining this[230] arrangement. To ensure that a similar problem does not arise[240] in future, please attend a meeting with the despatch clerk[250] in my office at nine forty-five on Monday morning.[260]

9 A letter accepting a decorator's estimate

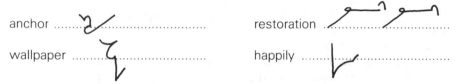

anchor ....

wallpaper ....

restoration ....

happily ....

Dear Mr Taylor, I refer to your visit to Anchor[10] Cottage earlier today when you gave me an estimate for[20] the decorating work needed in this property once the builders[30] have completed their restoration work. My husband and I accept[40] your estimate of five hundred pounds and confirm the following[50] points. The work on the dining and living rooms should[60] begin on 2nd October and be completed by 7th October.[70] You will then paper the kitchen with the design of[80] wallpaper chosen today, and by 10th October you will begin[90] work on the study and main bedroom on the first[100] floor. Decoration of the remaining three bedrooms on the second[110] floor will be completed by 3rd November. White gloss paint[120] will be used on all the woodwork, and the walls[130] will be papered as already agreed. As we will not[140] be moving into the cottage uuuntil all the
work is[150] done, the key will be available from the builders, Hope[160] and Mills of number six, Sea View Road. You may[170] keep the key to the property and we will then[180] collect it from you on 3rd November. You will recall[190] that we spoke about the possibility of your painting the[200] outside of the property in the spring of next year,[210] and for this you

quote a price of four hundred[220] pounds. We have considered this estimate and feel that if[230] you will include in this price the painting of the[240] summerhouse, we will happily agree to this sum. We would[250] welcome your very early comments. With kind regards, Yours sincerely[260]

10 A welcoming speech at an annual city show

rewarded ....

commercial ....

bee-keeping ....

conjunction ....

schedule ....

Welcome to the Fortieth Annual City Show being held once[10] again in Cooper's Field in the beautiful parkland behind the[20] castle. This year we are confident that the many months[30] of planning will be well rewarded by a show of[40] which our city can be very proud. As usual, we[50] will have attractions for all ages. In the main tent[60] you will find the commercial exhibitors. Their wonderful displays of[70] cut flowers, plants and vegetables are a joy to behold.[80] If you were privileged to see the City Council's display[90] last year, you will appreciate the care and attention that[100] is required to achieve such a marvellous spectacle, and you[110] will certainly not wish to miss this year's display which,[120] I promise you, will be even more spectacular. Exhibits at[130] the show will include flower arrangements, painting, bee-keeping, cookery,[140] horticulture, wine-making and many other interesting crafts. Special classes[150] for children under five are being introduced in this year's[160] show. Experts in many fields will be on hand to[170] answer any questions you may have. Catalogues and information leaflets[180] on many topics can be picked up free of charge.[190] As in previous years, the City Council is organizing the[200] show in conjunction with the Horticultural Society, whose members and[210] officers prepare the schedule, provide stewards and arrange the judging[220] of the amateur classes. There is a large fairground where[230] mums and dads can leave their children in safety while[240] they look at the exhibits. Your support is much appreciated[250] and contributes greatly to the continuing success of the show.[260]

Section Eleven
280-word passages

1 A letter from an investment consultant

portion ....   as far as ....

remainder ....   income tax ....

Dear Miss Brown, Thank you for your recent letter in[10] which you asked me for advice on how to invest[20] twenty thousand pounds to the best possible advantage. I note[30] that you have recently retired from work, that you have[40] no mortgage or other big financial commitments, and that the[50] income from your two pensions will be more than adequate[60] for your everyday needs. It would appear, therefore, that we[70] could consider using a portion of the money to buy[80] carefully selected shares which offer good prospects of a high[90] return on a short-term investment. However, in view of[100] the risk that is always present when purchasing such shares,[110] I think that not more than five thousand pounds should[120] be spent in this way. As far as the remainder[130] of the money is concerned, it would seem sensible to[140] opt for the security offered by either a building society[150] account or National Savings Certificates. Interest on the former is,[160] as you will probably know, paid after deduction of income[170] tax at the standard rate; in the latter case, however,[180] no tax is payable. At the moment I have no[190] knowledge of your position with regard to tax liability, and[200] would not wish to advise you further until I have[210] the necessary information. Perhaps it would be best if we[220] had a meeting to discuss the matter thoroughly. If it[230] would be convenient for you to come to this office,[240] please telephone my secretary to make an appointment. Alternatively, I[250] would be quite willing to visit you at your home[260] at any time and on any day suitable to you,[270] including Saturday and Sunday. Yours sincerely, James Porter, Investment Consultant[280]

2 Fast-food takeaways and continental restaurants

fast-food ....   outnumbered ....

beefburger ....   pizza ....

chop-suey ....   pineapple ....

In a large city it is possible to find a[10] vast range of restaurants and fast-food takeaways. The traditional[20] British fish and chip shops are being outnumbered by the[30] ever-increasing number of beefburger houses and pizza parlours which[40] are appearing all over the country. If you do not[50] feel like going out to eat on a cold wet[60] evening, it is possible to phone these establishments and place[70] your order. Within twenty minutes your supper will arrive at[80] your doorstep, freshly cooked and piping hot to enjoy in[90] the comfort of your own home. There is no need[100] to travel across land and sea for the magical taste[110] of the Orient. Chinese, Indian and Cantonese restaurants, to name[120] but a few, can now be added to the list[130] of Continental restaurants available. They provide the opportunity to savour[140] top-quality exotic dishes at reasonable prices. Chop-suey, stuffed[150] pineapple with roast duck, prawns with cashew nuts and chow-[160] mein are a few of the Chinese dishes available. The[170] restaurants are of traditional decor, and provide an ideal setting[180] for a celebration party or a romantic dinner for two.[190] Opening hours are from midday to three p.m. and seven[200] p.m. till midnight. For the figure conscious and keep-fit[210] fanatics, health-food bars are at hand. Wholemeal bread, brown[220] rice salad, sea-food platters and vegetable dishes are available[230] for the vegetarian members of the community. Personally, I am[240] quite happy to prepare and eat a home-cooked meal[250] such as steak and kidney pie with mixed vegetables, potatoes[260] and gravy, to be followed by freshly baked apple tart[270] and custard, in the relaxed atmosphere of my own home.[280]

3 A letter about fitting a bathroom suite

good enough ......⏝.......................   bidet ...... 6⁻.....................

integral ....~𝓍 𝓎.............................   whether or not ⌣⌐ ....

Dear Sir, May I thank you for being good enough[10] to send one of your plumbers out so promptly last[20] Thursday. He spotted and corrected the fault in my hot-[30] water system very quickly. I am pleased to say that[40] following his visit, the system has given no trouble at[50] all. While he was here I discussed with him the[60] possibility of having a new bathroom suite installed. He told[70] me that not only would your firm be able to[80] carry out the necessary plumbing work, but you would also[90] be in a position to supply the suite itself. Perhaps[100] if I give you an indication of my requirements, you[110] could send more information. The suite I would prefer will[120] consist of a corner bath, a wash basin on pedestal[130] stand and a low-level water closet. The colour would[140] be either light green or plain white. I would also[150] like to consider the possibility of having a bidet installed,[160] subject to there being adequate space in the bathroom to[170] accommodate this. An electric shower would also be necessary. However,[180] I would prefer an integral shower unit as opposed to[190] having the unit installed over the bath. Ideally, I would[200] appreciate a visit from one of your company representatives. Perhaps[210] he could bring with him catalogues depicting the various styles[220] and colours of the bathroom fittings you are able to[230] supply. It would also be necessary for him to take[240] measurements of the bathroom in order to determine whether or[250] not the items selected would fit into the room. Please[260] do not hesitate to write or telephone to arrange the[270] most suitable time for your representative to call. Yours faithfully[280]

4 Home wine-making

delicious ....⌐..............................   strawberry ....𝒷...........

dandelion .....⌐..................   chemists ....𝒸ₒ...............

end-product ....ℎ......ℎ...........
                                        𝓉𝒸

A hobby which seems to be growing in popularity is[10] that of home wine-making. A wide variety of wine-[20] making kits are available in the shops, also books which[30] give hints and advice on how to achieve good results.[40] The base for wine can come from sources such as[50] flowers, vegetables and fruit. Why not try brewing a delicious[60] strawberry wine. When the strawberries are in season they are[70] not too expensive to buy. Better still, why not enjoy[80] a day out with your family or friends and pick[90] your own. Many small farms encourage the public to go[100] along and pick their own fruit. Armed with a straw[110] punnet, you can select the best berries and buy them[120] at prices well below what you would have to pay[130] in a shop. An even cheaper and easier ingredient to[140] use as the base for your wine grows wild in[150] your garden. It is the dandelion. The experts say that[160] an excellent dry wine can be brewed from dandelions. However,[170] if your tastebuds shiver at the thought of dandelion wine[180] and you do not wish to go fruit picking, there[190] are many varieties of wine bases available in tins, which[200] can be purchased from specialist shops of the larger chemists[210] and give full instructions for use. As already mentioned, many[220] varieties are available: for instance, the deep red claret or[230] the light sparkling table wine. However, if you fancy the[240] idea of making your own wine at home, you should[250] bear in mind that the end-product may be a[260] very potent drink. It may also contain a high proportion[270] of sugar, which is not good news for weight watchers.[280]

5 A circular letter about car telephones

features ....   useful ....

freepost ....

Dear Sir or Madam, If you spend a lot of[10] time driving around in your car, you really should consider[20] the advantages of having a car telephone. You can turn[30] your car into a mobile office and it will cost[40] you less than a pound a day. When you think[50] of the business you might lose while you are in[60] your car, we are sure you will agree this is[70] a small price to pay. We believe our phone is[80] the best on the market. It has many special features,[90] including a memory which holds the fifty numbers you need[100] most often. Think how useful it would be to be[110] in touch with clients and business contacts while on the[120] road. Our price for a five-year rental scheme is[130] only six pounds a week. If you prefer to purchase,[140] we can let you know the cash price. If you[150] would like more information, fill in the coupon and send[160] it to us using the freepost address. Please indicate whether[170] you would like us to send our brochure or whether[180] you would like us to contact you to arrange a[190] demonstration. Alternatively, you can ring your local office. The numbers[200] are listed above. The phone will be installed by our[210] own engineers, and our excellent service is always available to[220] give you complete peace of mind. We already have over[230] forty thousand satisfied customers all over the country. We are[240] sure you will agree that the time has come for[250] you to join them. This amazing offer can only be[260] maintained while existing stocks last, so do not hesitate to[270] write or phone for additional information without delay. Yours faithfully[280]

6 A hotel chain gives details of conference facilities

conference facilities ....   hard day's work ....

it is necessary ....

More and more companies are coming aware of the need[10] for training programmes to ensure that all their employees are[20] as efficient as possible. A good training programme needs to[30] be planned well in advance, and one of the most[40] important aspects to be considered is where the training is[50] to take place. Some training, of course, can be done[60] within the company itself but sometimes it is a good[70] idea to get away to different surroundings. This is where[80] we can help you. We have hotels all over the[90] country, some in cities and near to large business centres,[100] and some in peaceful countryside. Each of them has excellent[110] conference facilities. We can provide lecture rooms which will contain[120] all the modern equipment you will need. You can also[130] choose as many meeting rooms as you like and these[140] can be whatever size you wish. Extra services such as[150] secretaries or telex are available should you require them. Whether[160] you are bringing ten employees or a hundred, we will[170] do everything possible to make your conference a success. After[180] a hard day's work, your staff will enjoy the first-[190] class service which is expected from our hotels. The meals,[200] of course, will be of a high standard and will[210] be served by our experienced staff. Every bedroom has its[220] own bathroom and is well furnished and very comfortable. Each[230] one contains a desk and reading lamp in case it[240] is necessary for work to be completed. Most hotels have[250] a swimming pool, and a relaxing swim before dinner makes[260] a welcome break. If you would like to know more[270] about how we can help, please ring our conference manager.[280]

7 A letter about marketing hand-made knitwear

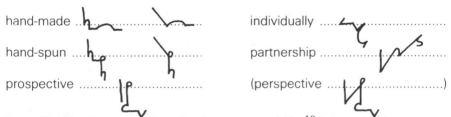

hand-made	individually
hand-spun	partnership
prospective	(perspective)

Dear Sir, I write to enquire whether you would be[10] interested in marketing my hand-made knitwear. I enclose photographs[20] of some of the garments I have made, which are[30] all individually designed. I am also enclosing some samples of[40] my work, which I should be pleased to have returned[50] when you have inspected them. I spin some of the[60] wool myself but this does take a long time so,[70] of course, hand-spun garments cost a lot more than[80] those made with commercially produced wool. I have indicated on[90] the reverse of the photographs whether the wool is hand-[100] spun. I normally produce one garment a week and I[110] do take orders for customers' own requirements. I state on[120] each garment the price I require for it and you[130] would, of course, be free to add whatever mark-up[140] you wish. If you took any orders for me I[150] should wish to give a price and have this agreed[160] before embarking on the project. I have a printed brochure[170] but it is not possible to give exact prices on[180] this, as each garment is so individual in pattern, size[190] and material, but I do show a price-band to[200] give prospective customers some idea. You will note that I[210] have my own woven labels indicating that the garment is[220] hand-knitted and, where appropriate, hand- spun. I already have[230] outlets in some tourist areas but I know how well[240] your village is catering for a growing number of visitors,[250] and I feel we could set up a small-scale[260] but profitable partnership. If you are at all interested in[270] stocking my goods, please let me know soon. Yours faithfully[280]

8 A letter to a book club

herewith ...... *[outline]* ......   diary ...... *[outline]* ......

unaware ...... *[outline]* ......

Dear Sirs, I am returning the book which you sent[10] me recently and hope very much that you will exchange[20] it for me. I appreciate the fact that I did[30] promise to take one book each quarter, but for some[40] reason or other I have missed the ordering date and[50] you have sent me the editor's choice which is of[60] no interest to me. I have completed an order form[70] and am sending it herewith. You will see that the[80] books I have indicated thereon are equal in value to[90] the book I am returning, so I would request your[100] co-operation in this instance. This is the first time since[110] I took out my membership with you that I have[120] missed sending in my order in time, and this arose[130] because I had been away from home for a few[140] weeks. I know I should write the closing date in[150] my diary as a reminder to send off my order,[160] but unfortunately I omitted to do this. I would like[170] to say how much I enjoy the books I receive[180] from your club. I have been a member now for[190] seven years, and each quarter I find something in your[200] catalogue which I would like to buy. The prices compare[210] very favourably with similar books I have looked at in[220] local bookshops, and I do like having my attention drawn[230] to new books, of which I might otherwise be unaware.[240] It is just unfortunate that on the only occasion I[250] have missed the closing date, the book you have sent[260] is unsuitable. I hope you will replace it and look[270] forward to receiving the books I have ordered. Yours faithfully[280]

9 The attractions of a holiday in Britain

Mediterranean ...... *[outline]* ......   picturesque ...... *[outline]* ......

language ...... *[outline]* ......   smuggler ...... *[outline]* ......

over-exposure ...... *[outline]* ......

Dear Client, If you are thinking about booking your annual[10] holiday, there are a number of points you perhaps ought[20] to consider before rushing to the travel agent to reserve[30] two weeks in the Mediterranean sun. Firstly, consider how much[40] – or how little – travelling you have done in your own[50] country. There are many beautiful parts of the British Isles,[60] and visiting them can make a holiday you will remember[70] for years to come. Have you been to the Lake[80] District and seen the deep lakes surrounded by hills and[90] mountains? Have you seen the picturesque villages of Sussex and[100] the rugged areas on the north-east coast? Have you[110] toured Scotland, a land of lowlands, highlands, rivers and islands?[120] Have you visited the castles of Wales or walked across[130] the wide beaches of Devon? Secondly, a holiday in Britain[140] will not involve you in the need to exchange currency,[150] buy medicines in case you are affected by the food[160] or the insects in the country you are visiting, or[170] learn another language. In addition, just think of the relief[180] at not having to wait for long hours at the[190] airport if your flight is delayed, and not having to[200] open your luggage to satisfy a Customs Officer that you[210] are not a smuggler. A third point you may wish[220] to consider is that, although a holiday in Britain may[230] not have the long hours of sunshine of a holiday[240] abroad, you will not have to worry about the effects[250] of over-exposure to fierce sunlight. If you agree with[260] us that a holiday in Britain has a lot to[270] commend it, why not contact us today. Yours faithfully, Director[280]

10 A letter about wedding anniversary celebrations

anniversary ....   extra ....

menus ....

Dear Mr Bramley, We confirm our telephone conversation today, booking[10] accommodation for the occasion of our Silver Wedding anniversary. My[20] wife and I require a double room with private facilities[30] on 11th, 12th, and 13th May and six double rooms[40] for the night of 11th May only. The cost of[50] these extra rooms should be added to our account, as[60] they will be for our guests at the private dinner[70] we wish to hold in your Emerald Room on Saturday,[80] 11th. We have had an opportunity to study your function[90] menus and wish our guests to be able to choose[100] from menus five and seven. Since our conversation, we have[110] spoken to two of our friends who will be travelling[120] some distance, so perhaps dinner could be served at twenty[130] hundred hours rather than at nineteen hundred hours? This will[140] give our friends the opportunity to relax for a while[150] after their long journey before the celebrations begin. My wife[160] particularly likes the idea of fresh carnations being provided for[170] the ladies of the party to wear, and we would[180] like the cost of this service to be included on[190] our account. Your suggestion that a three-piece band could[200] play in the corner of the suite during dinner is[210] greatly appreciated, and the cost of this too should be[220] added to our account. One of our friends wishes to[230] bring her dog with her, and we have been asked[240] to enquire if this is acceptable to you and if[250] you have any restrictions on where he may be kept[260] during her stay? We thank you for your help and[270] look forward to meeting you on the 11th. Yours sincerely[280]

Section Twelve
300-word passages

1 A personal letter from an aunt

mentioned ....   the other day ....

at present ....

Dear Margaret, I was very pleased to receive your letter,[10] and delighted to hear that you have passed all your[20] examinations and have been accepted as a student at my[30] local college. I do hope this means that we shall[40] see more of each other than has been possible over[50] the last few years. You mentioned in your letter that[60] it is proving difficult to find suitable accommodation in this[70] area. I am not surprised. Whenever I go into town,[80] I find it full of young people and I am[90] sure most of them are students. I wonder if you[100] would consider sharing a flat with another girl of about[110] your age? If so, then I think I can help[120] you. One of my neighbours owns the flat and he[130] mentioned to me only the other day that he was[140] looking for a suitable tenant. The one he has at[150] present used to share with her sister, but she got[160] married a few weeks ago and has set up home[170] with her husband in another part of the country. My[180] neighbour says that his tenant – her name is, I believe,[190] Carol Harper – is a very pleasant and quiet girl who[200] works in an office in the town centre. She is[210] also studying for an Open University degree so I imagine[220] she would be the kind of girl you would get[230] on with. The flat is situated on the same side[240] of town as the college, so you would have no[250] travel problems. If you are interested in the flat, perhaps[260] you would ring my neighbour as soon as possible. His[270] name is Charles Manning and his number is South Milford[280] 6242. Give my love to your parents[290] and, of course, to young Timothy. Much love, Aunt Mabel[300]

2 A letter about accident insurance

drastically ....   stressful ....

inexpensive ....   serious consideration ....

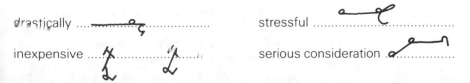

Dear Customer, As a highly valued customer of this company,[10] I am
writing to introduce you to an insurance scheme[20] that could prove to be
more important than all your[30] other insurance policies combined. The
scheme is designed to give[40] cover in the event of an accident to yourself
or[50] a member of your family. If you take just a[60] few minutes to consider
the insurance cover you already have,[70] you will discover you have
protection for your home, its[80] contents and your car. Yet what about
yourself, the most[90] valuable asset you have? Most of us think that
accidents[100] only ever happen to other people. Unfortunately, this is
not[110] the case. Fate can, and often does, strike at any[120] time, and to all
sorts of people. When an accident[130] does happen you may find your
income is drastically reduced,[140] yet the usual household bills continue
to come in. If[150] you take action now, before the worst happens, this
stressful[160] financial situation can be avoided. Our Accident Plan gives
cover[170] which is very simple and inexpensive. It has been designed[180] to
provide high lump-sum cash benefits, plus extra financial[190] help should
you need an extended stay in hospital. The[200] formalities are minimal,
no medical is necessary and there is[210] no upper age limit. There is just
one simple application[220] form to be completed, of which acceptance is
guaranteed if[230] you apply before 1st September. Premiums are modest
and are[240] paid monthly. You will receive your policy documents to
examine[250] for up to twenty-one days without obligation in the[260]
privacy of your own home. If you decide not to[270] accept the Plan, simply
return the policy within twenty-one[280] days and you will owe nothing.
We do hope you[290] will give your serious consideration to this offer.
Yours faithfully[300]

3 The office receptionist

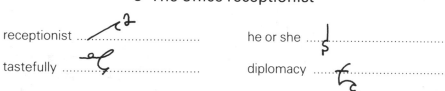

receptionist ....

he or she ....

tastefully ....

diplomacy ....

The first person a visitor to a company will meet[10] is the receptionist. It
is obvious, then, that the receptionist[20] has the important task of
creating the first impression – which,[30] of course, must be a good one.
Firstly, the visitor[40] will see the receptionist and the area in which he[50]
or she works. A pleasing appearance together with a clean[60] tidy office
are needed to help create the very first[70] favourable impression. Usually,
a few plants tastefully arranged in the[80] reception area will make it look
more attractive. Secondly, the[90] caller will speak to the receptionist, and
the manner and[100] attitude used when replying should be polite and
friendly. Nobody[110] enjoys entering a strange building only to be growled

at,[120] or even ignored, by the staff. Having welcomed the caller[130] and found out the purpose of his or her visit,[140] the receptionist should contact the person who can best deal[150] with the caller. If the person the caller needs to[160] see is not immediately available, this should be explained. Never[170] leave a visitor just to wait and wonder what is[180] happening. If the waiting time turns out to be lengthy,[190] periodic contact should be made with the visitor explaining the[200] reason for the delay, apologizing for it, and perhaps offering[210] some kind of refreshment. Of course, it may be the[220] case that the caller is not welcome. Some people will[230] just walk into the office and demand to be seen.[240] If the person they wish to see refuses the request,[250] great tact and diplomacy should be used. Perhaps it could[260] be suggested that the caller states his business and makes[270] an appointment to see the staff member in question. The[280] receptionist's task is not only to receive visitors, but this[290] is probably the most important of his or her duties.[300]

4 A letter of reference for Miss Ann Clark

personality ....   communicate ....

applicants ....   competence ....

Dear Mr Williams, Thank you for your letter of 6th[10] March requesting a reference for Miss Ann Clark. I am[20] very pleased to give you the following information. Miss Clark[30] joined our firm three years ago as a shorthand-typist.[40] She had just completed a course at her local college[50] and had passed all her examinations. Her tutor told us[60] that she had been an excellent student. During her first[70] two years with us she worked for five different people[80] and gained a good knowledge of the firm. Her work[90] was always accurate and well presented, and she took an[100] interest in everything she did. She was completely reliable and[110] had very little time off through sickness. Last year we[120] were pleased to be able to promote her to private[130] secretary to the sales manager. Since then her work has[140] become much more varied: for example, she has to take[150] minutes of meetings and organize the travel arrangements for her[160] boss. These are often long trips abroad which involve a[170] great deal of careful planning. On occasions, she also has[180] to deal with visitors to her department, some of whom[190] are very important clients. She has a most pleasant personality[200] and is able to communicate well with people of all[210] levels. In her present position, she has a junior clerk[220] to help with the work, and we have such confidence[230] in her judgement that we allow her to interview applicants[240] for junior posts and to recommend the person she thinks[250] most suitable. She is responsible for giving a certain amount[260] of training and she does this work with competence. We[270] should be very sorry indeed to lose Miss Clark, but[280] we do understand her genuine reasons for wanting to move[290] to your part of the country. Yours sincerely, Office Manager[300]

5 Organizing successful business meetings

chairperson ....   in such a way ....

paperwork ....

Meetings seem to take up more and more time in[10] business today. Because of this, it is important to make[20] sure that the time is well spent and that the[30] meeting does serve a really useful purpose. It is absolutely[40] vital to have a good chairperson. He or she should[50] be able to control the meeting in such a way[60] that there is plenty of discussion without any waste of[70] time. The size of the committee should be carefully looked[80] at. If it is too large, it may be very[90] hard to get any kind of agreement. On the other[100] hand, it must be large enough to include all the[110] people who have the knowledge needed to discuss the matters[120] on the agenda. The problem of size can sometimes be[130] solved by having several small working parties who are given[140] a particular topic to investigate. When they finish their work,[150] they can report their findings to the full committee. Another[160] important point is to ensure that every member fully understands[170] why the committee was set up in the first place.[180] They should know exactly what they are trying to achieve.[190] It is also necessary to know the rules under which[200] the committee works. These can vary, depending on whether the[210] meeting is formal or informal, and new members should always[220] have the rules explained to them before their first meeting.[230] It is obvious that all the necessary paperwork needs to[240] be prepared with great care. The agenda and minutes must[250] be absolutely accurate and any extra reports that may be[260] needed must be available at the meeting or sent out[270] to the members in advance. The date of the next[280] meeting should be fixed in good time, so that everyone[290] can make sure they will be free to attend it.[300]

6 A report by the chairman of a building group

substantial ....   emphasis ....

in full agreement ....   enthusiasm ....

Ladies and Gentlemen, The past year has been one of[10] substantial progress in the development of the Group. Pre-tax[20] profit increased by thirty-nine per cent, and turnover in[30] the period increased by thirty per cent to twenty million[40] pounds, with a total of five hundred and ten dwellings[50] completed. A dividend increase for the full year of eighteen[60] per cent is recommended. At the end of the financial[70] year, the Group had funds on deposit of two million[80] pounds compared with loans of one point seven million pounds[90] at the end of the previous financial year. This favourable[100] cash position results from the funds received last July from[110] the rights issue, which was fully taken up. This put[120] the Group in a strong cash position, the full benefits[130] of which will not be felt until next year. The[140] Board are of the opinion that continued emphasis on good[150] marketing, and excellence of design based on traditional principles, is[160] important. Our staff are in full agreement with this approach,[170] and their enthusiasm shows itself in loyalty and real effort.[180] I would like at this stage to express my sincere[190] thanks to all members of staff who have contributed to[200] our growing success over the years. The level of sales[210] continues to rise and the number of new housing developments[220] we are launching creates an encouraging picture. In anticipation of[230] the availability of funds from the rights issue, we stepped[240] up our land acquisition programme and we currently have a[250] bank of about two thousand plots – a considerable increase over[260] last year. The future growth of our Group is well[270] provided for by this larger land bank and our increased[280] financial strength. Bearing in mind the Group's achievements over the[290] last five years, I believe a successful year lies ahead.[300]

7 A speech at a public meeting

landlord .... ⟨shorthand⟩   developer .... ⟨shorthand⟩

caterers ....

Ladies and Gentlemen, This meeting has been called so that[10] we can discuss what action to take following the threatened[20] closure of our village inn. As you are all aware,[30] this is the only public meeting place in our small[40] village. Unlike the majority of rural communities, we have no[50] hall in which to meet or hold functions, and until[60] now we have relied on the accommodation provided by the[70] inn, for which we have always been extremely grateful to[80] the landlord. Now that the inn has been sold to[90] a developer, who will very likely apply for planning permission[100] to erect houses on the site, we must decide what[110] action can be taken in an attempt to save our[120] only meeting place. Many residents have expressed the fear that[130] village life will disappear altogether. We have already lost our[140] shop and our school, and if we lose our only[150] inn there will be no community spirit left. There would[160] appear to be several options open to us. First of[170] all, we can object individually to any proposal which is[180] put forward to demolish the inn and build housing units[190] on the site. This will need to be done quickly[200] once the proposal is published. Secondly, a number of residents[210] have indicated that they would be willing to put up[220] the money to buy the property back from the developer[230] if planning permission is refused. They would then continue to[240] run the inn as a joint venture. Another idea is[250] to convert it into a community centre, letting out rooms[260] for such functions as receptions and conferences. There are good[270] outside caterers nearby and, as the setting of the building[280] is so attractive, there should be no difficulty in marketing[290] these facilities. Now I would like to hear your views.[300]

8   Advice on buying an engagement ring

engaged ....

grandparents ....

great-grandparents ....

ornate ....

Getting engaged should be a happy occasion when the families[10] and close friends of both parties celebrate the forthcoming marriage[20] of two people. An engagement should be regarded as a[30] commitment for the rest of your life, and it is[40] appropriate that most couples choose to mark this enduring relationship[50] by choosing a ring set with diamonds, because diamonds are[60] reputed to last for ever. More than three hundred thousand[70] diamond engagement rings are bought each year in the United[80] Kingdom at a cost of over fifty million pounds; but[90] before you and your partner spend part of this fifty[100] million pounds on your engagement ring, consider the following advice.[110] If you buy a ring set with good-quality precious[120] stones it will appreciate in value, but only after a[130] number of years, so do consider an antique ring. Older[140] rings which belonged to our grandparents and great-grandparents are[150] often set with less expensive stones in ornate settings and[160] these certainly will rise in value. However, if it has[170] to be a diamond, buy the best-quality stones you[180] can afford, in a simple setting, and remember you can[190] have the stones reset at a later date when you[200] may have more money to spare. Choose a reliable jeweller[210] or antique dealer, and once you have bought the ring[220] look after it. It is important to insure the item,[230] and some jewellers will offer the first year's insurance free[240] of charge. Do remember to continue the insurance and to[250] increase the insured value of the ring by ten or[260] twenty per cent each year. It is also wise to[270] have the ring cleaned every two or three years, and[280] to ask the jeweller to check the setting to ensure[290] that no stones are loose and likely to be lost.[300]

9 Being a member of a book club

introductory ...*(shorthand)*...   monthly ...*(shorthand)*...

forgetful ...*(shorthand)*...

Do you belong to a book club? If not, have[10] you ever considered becoming a member? You will receive the[20] offer of purchasing hard-backed books at discount prices on[30] a wide range of subjects from fiction to gardening, beauty[40] care to cooking, fortune telling to decorating, and many more.[50] There are, however, certain things of which you should be[60] aware before you complete the application form. Most clubs offer[70] you up to four introductory books at greatly reduced prices[80] – and sometimes these are as low as fifty pence each[90] – in an attempt to entice you to join. Before you[100] become too impressed with this offer, read the small print[110] on the advertisement. You may have to agree to take[120] a book from the club every month during the first[130] year of membership, although some firms require you to take[140] only four books during your first year. Think carefully about[150] the commitment to take a book every month; the choice[160] may be great but do you really want this financial[170] obligation? Most clubs send you a monthly catalogue of the[180] books available, included in which is their special Book of[190] the Month which you will usually be sent and will[200] have to pay for unless you remember to inform the[210] club that you do not wish to have it. For[220] the forgetful person this can be difficult, and you may[230] receive a book you did not wish to purchase. So,[240] if you know exactly what you are entering into, you[250] will have the opportunity to purchase books on interesting subjects[260] for yourself and your family, and will also be able[270] to shop for presents for friends in the comfort of[280] your home. It is also an opportunity to develop an[290] interest in a subject that is quite new to you.[300]

10 Buying second-hand cars

comforting ...*(shorthand)*...   self-esteem ...*(shorthand)*...

up-market ...*(shorthand)*...

These days it seems that more and more people are[10] able to enjoy the benefits of a company car, but[20] there are still some of us who own our own[30] and, in most cases, that means a second-hand vehicle.[40] It can be frustrating to read the motoring columns in[50] newspapers where the latest models of new cars are reviewed,[60] but it is comforting to realize that there are some[70] very real advantages in buying a second-hand car. Driving[80] a brand new car with the current registration to advertise[90] your status may give you a boost in terms of[100] self-esteem, but you are hit pretty hard in your[110] pocket as soon as you take delivery. Apart from a[120] very few specialist vehicles, made in small runs, new cars[130] lose value as soon as they are driven off the[140] garage forecourt. The average family model, driven for about three[150] thousand miles, will have lost about a quarter of its[160] new value, so it makes good financial sense to buy[170] a used car if you have to pay for the[180] vehicle yourself or if you wish to move up-market[190] to a more recent model. Great care should be taken[200] when looking for a used car for sale, because not[210] all second-hand cars are the bargains they seem to[220] be and not all garages dealing in such cars are[230] equally reliable. Most of us have heard horror stories related[240] to people who have been unfortunate enough to have bought[250] unsafe cars from shady dealers. If you find a car[260] that you like, but may be unsure of its true[270] condition beneath the showroom polish, it is a good idea[280] to pay an expert to check the vehicle for you.[290] Peace of mind is worth more than a few pounds.[300]

Section Thirteen
320-word passages

1 Photography

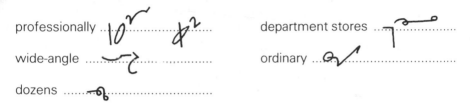

professionally ....

wide-angle ....

dozens ....

department stores ....

ordinary ....

For many years, professionally taken family and child portraits have[10] been given and accepted as delightful Christmas presents. At one[20] time only the very wealthy could afford to have professional[30] portraits taken. Today this is no longer the case. Although[40] costs are now lower, picture quality is higher than ever.[50] It is easy for a photographic sitting to be fitted[60] into a shopping trip, as there are many studios in[70] towns and cities. Over the Christmas period large department stores[80] play host to travelling portrait studios and offer special discounts[90] to attract customers. Mothers of young children are always keen[100] to have photographs of their offspring to show off to[110] friends and relatives. Photography has become a very popular hobby[120] with many people from all walks of life. Most start[130] with a simple camera until they find it limits their[140] ability to take excellent photographs. A good camera may cost[150] at least one hundred pounds, but it could have the[160] advantage of allowing the user to change the lens so[170] that a good photograph can be taken in almost any[180] situation. A wide-angle lens will cover a much wider[190] area than an ordinary lens, while a telephoto lens will[200] bring an object closer. Camera clubs are of great benefit[210] to those wishing to improve their skills, enter photographic competitions,[220] or sell their pictures. To most people a camera provides,[230] above all, the opportunity to record special events. Dozens of[240] cameras can usually be seen and heard clicking away in[250] the hands of guests at weddings and Christenings. Nearly everyone[260] takes a camera on their annual holiday abroad, where dozens[270] of snaps will be taken on the beach, in the[280] bars, hotels and swimming pools. We all look forward to[290] seeing our holiday pictures when they have been developed and[300] printed –

even when they are far from being perfect. We[310] also take great delight
in boring other people with them![320]

2 Young people of today and yesterday

teenagers .... *(shorthand symbol)* ....   youngsters ..*(shorthand symbol)*............

supermarket ...*(shorthand symbol)*............   earrings ....*(shorthand symbol)*............

People of my age, who were teenagers thirty or forty[10] years ago, are
often amazed at the clothes worn by[20] some of today's youngsters, and at
the things they do[30] to their hair and faces. The other day I saw[40] a
young couple shopping in a supermarket. She was wearing[50] black boots,
black tights with holes in them, a short[60] black skirt and a black pullover
at least three sizes[70] too large with holes to match the tights. Her hair-[80]
style was impossible to describe and her earrings were the[90] biggest I
have ever seen. Her face was painted silver[100] with two red lines on each
cheek. He was wearing[110] black boots, too, which looked as though they
had once[120] belonged to a cowboy. His tattered jeans failed by a[130] good
six inches to reach his ankles, and his black[140] leather jacket was
adorned with at least fifty metal badges.[150] As far as I could tell, he had
not a[160] hair on his head, which was topped by a black[170] bowler hat that
had seen better days – probably in the[180] City of London. His face was
made up in what[190] I took to be the style of a Red Indian[200] on the
warpath. When I was young the girls usually[210] wore neatly pressed
blouses and skirts, nylon stockings and polished[220] black or brown shoes.
Most of them had one or[230] two dresses which were reserved for special
occasions. The minimum[240] of make-up was used: just a little lipstick
and[250] a touch of rouge. The boys wore trousers and sports[260] jackets:
only more fortunate ones had a suit for special[270] occasions. It never
crossed anyone's mind that members of the[280] male sex should use make-
up or paint their faces[290] unless, of course, they were appearing in a
theatrical production.[300] I wonder what the couple I saw in the
supermarket[310] will think of young people thirty or forty years hence.[320]

3 Shorthand speed-building

vocabulary ......*(shorthand symbol)*............   at the end of the day ....*(shorthand symbol)*............

gradually ....*(shorthand symbol)*............

One of the best ways to build up your writing[10] speed is to write the same
short passage over and[20] over again, until you find that you have reached

the[30] stage where you no longer have to think about how[40] to write any of the words in it. If you[50] do this with several short passages you will soon build[60] up a vocabulary of words you can write without any[70] conscious thought, and when those words crop up in a[80] new passage you will not hesitate over them. Gradually, the[90] number of outlines which you are writing for the first[100] time will reduce until you reach the point where only[110] the occasional rare word causes you to hesitate and, eventually,[120] even the outlines for those rare words can be written[130] with no difficulty. When you begin speed-building, it is[140] particularly important to master the very common little words such[150] as I, you, he, she, it, we, they, at, from,[160] for, if, by, what, which, when, why, with, where and[170] who. These are words which will crop up time after[180] time, no matter what you are writing about. It is[190] also important to read as much shorthand as possible, especially[200] your own notes, because this will help to fix the[210] outlines in your mind and make it easier to recall[220] them when you have to write them at speed. Speed-[230] building is not as easy as some people seem to[240] think, but if you get off to a good start[250] by learning the theory and practising your shorthand on every[260] possible occasion, there is no reason why you should not[270] reach a useful speed in a very short time. At[280] the end of the day, perhaps eight per cent of[290] the speed you have will be due to the amount[300] of practice you put in, while some twenty per cent[310] will be due to your 'natural ability' to write quickly.[320]

4 A letter about booking hotel rooms to accommodate a conference

advertising agency ....   overhead projector ....

refreshments ....

Dear Sir, I am writing in my capacity as secretary[10] to the managing director of a local advertising agency, namely[20] Hillcrest Limited. We are currently trying to make arrangements for[30] a conference meeting. The meeting is to be a large[40] one, with some three hundred people expected to attend, and[50] we are unable to hold the conference in our company[60] offices because of a lack of space and facilities. We[70] would, if possible, like to book the use of a[80] suite of rooms in your hotel. The main room in[90] which the conference would be held should be large enough[100] to seat three hundred people. It should also be fitted[110] with at least six electric sockets to allow us to[120] use an overhead projector together with other related equipment. At[130] least three alternative rooms should also be made available to[140] allow for rest periods or private discussions to take place.[150] The conference is to be held over a three-day[160] period, and the rooms will be required for the whole[170] of that time. About sixty of the expected guests will[180] be travelling some distance to attend the conference and will[190] need accommodation on a bed-and-breakfast basis for two[200] nights. The rooms allocated to them should have private bathing[210] or washing facilities. We would be most obliged if your[220] catering staff could accommodate us regarding meals and refreshments. On[230] each of the three days, morning coffee will be required[240] at eleven o'clock, a buffet lunch at one o'clock, and[250] afternoon tea and biscuits at three o'clock, to be served[260] in the dining area. Please could you let me know[270] as soon as possible if the booking can be made[280] firm. The anticipated dates for the conference are from the[290] 8th to the 10th of July inclusive. Please do not[300] hesitate to contact me should you require further details. I[310] look forward to hearing from you very soon. Yours faithfully[320]

5 The life of the market trader

illusions ....   imagination ....

potential ....   influence ....

torrential ....

Whilst walking around a local market on a hot day[10] last summer, I thought how lucky the traders were to[20] have such a pleasant working environment. They stood by their[30] stalls chatting with would-be customers and enjoying the sunshine.[40] What an easy and enjoyable occupation they seemed to have.[50] However, as I questioned some of them my illusions began[60] to disappear. Their working life was not quite so simple[70] as it appeared. Depending on the distance to be covered[80] to reach the market, the day could start as early[90] as five in the morning. Before actually setting off for[100] market, the vans need to be loaded up with the[110] goods. On arrival, the stall has to be erected before[120] unloading takes place. I am told that on icy cold[130] mornings it is essential to wear gloves for this task,[140] to prevent your skin from sticking to the steel bars[150] which make up the stall. Once the stall is erected,[160] unloading is done and the wares are then displayed on[170] the stall to their best advantage. Care and imagination are[180] needed for this task. Care, because the traders have to[190] contend with all kinds of weather. Strong winds and driving[200] rain could ruin their stock. Imagination, because the goods must[210] be displayed in such a manner that they catch the[220] eye of the potential customer. This work must be completed[230] by approximately nine o'clock to enable the traders to give[240] their full attention to the customer, commonly called 'the punter'.[250] Of course, the trader never knows in advance whether it[260] is going to be worth his while attending market. He[270] may on occasion work a twelve- or fourteen-hour day[280] for little or no reward. Once again, the weather conditions[290] have a strong influence on this. For instance, not many[300] people will shop at a local market in torrential rain,[310] when they could be warm and dry inside a supermarket.[320]

6 A letter about free telephone calls to an insurance company

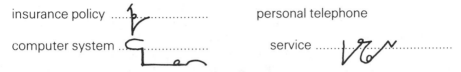

insurance policy ....

computer system ....

personal telephone

service ....

Dear Mr Brown, Thank you for your recent enquiry about[10] taking out a new insurance policy with us for your[20] home and contents. We note that your present policy is[30] almost due for renewal, and shall be very pleased to[40] prepare a quotation for you. However, we know that most[50] people prefer to have a chance to discuss their exact[60] requirements, and to make sure the policy meets all their[70] needs. For this reason we provide a personal telephone service.[80] If you would like to ring the number at the[90] top of this letter, you will be connected to my[100] department. You can call on any weekday from eight in[110] the morning until eight at night, and the call will[120] be free of charge. When you ring, would you please[130] quote the reference number shown above. This will enable any[140] of my staff to discuss your policy with you. The[150] details you have kindly given us have been entered on[160] our computer system, and my staff will be able to[170] have these in front of them as soon as your[180] call is received. I am sure you will find it[190] worth your while to contact us. There is of course[200] no obligation upon you to accept our quotation but, if[210] you do decide to go ahead, we can arrange to[220] provide immediate cover. In fact, a cover note will be[230] put in the post to you straight away and there[240] is no need for you to make any payment until[250] you receive it. You can be quite certain that your[260] home and contents are covered from the moment you put[270] the phone down. We do hope you will take this[280] opportunity to have a free personal discussion with us. Our[290] staff are all experts, and you will find them both[300] friendly and efficient. We look forward to hearing from you[310] in the very near future. Yours sincerely, John Green, Manager[320]

7 A letter from a headmaster about the annual Sports Day

obstacle race ....

children ....

Dear Parent, We are arranging to hold our annual Sports[10] Day this year on Thursday, 16th July. This is the[20] last day of the summer term, and will make a[30] very pleasant ending to the school year. We are planning[40] to hold all the usual races, plus one or two[50] new ones which we think will be fun. We have[60] been careful to make sure that every child takes part[70] in at least two of the events, so that the[80] whole school is involved. The first race will take place[90] at three o'clock, but the school will be open from[100] two o'clock. We hope you will get here early so[110] that you can look at the displays. In addition to[120] the general work on show in the classrooms, there will[130] be a special exhibition of the children's painting, drawing and[140] pottery. They have produced some particularly good work this year,[150] and we are sure you will be impressed by what[160] they have done. After the last race has finished and[170] the prizes have been given out, the afternoon will end[180] at five o'clock with a short programme of songs and[190] dances by our five-year-old pupils. I have been[200] watching them prepare for this and I know you will[210] enjoy seeing them perform. I should like to remind you[220] that one of the most popular events of the afternoon[230] is the obstacle race for adults. If you would like[240] to take part in this, remember to bring suitable clothing[250] and shoes with you. The children always enjoy watching their[260] parents going round the course, and this year the teachers[270] have agreed to take part as well. As usual, we[280] could do with some extra help on the day. If[290] you think you could spare a little time to help[300] with the refreshments, or to mark out the tracks, perhaps[310] you would let me know. Yours truly, Peter Cook, Headmaster[320]

8 A letter about a private hotel for sale

with reference to your letter ....   en-suite ....

renovated ....

Dear Mrs Lane, With reference to your letter of 1st[10] June, in which you state that you wish to buy[20] premises suitable for use as a guest house, we have[30] a property on our books at the present time which[40] we think will meet your requirements. The property is at[50] present being run as a small private hotel. It is[60] situated right on the sea-front in very attractive gardens[70] totalling about a third of an acre. There are nine[80] bedrooms, all with hot and cold water. Some of these[90] would lend themselves to conversion to en-suite bathrooms if[100] you should think this desirable. There is a separate flat[110] for staff on the first floor. On the ground floor[120] there is a very large and well-lit dining room[130] and a residents' lounge. The reception area is spacious, and[140] a curving staircase leads from it to the first floor.[150] The hotel has obtained a fire certificate from the Local[160] Authority. There is an external iron staircase to allow escape[170] from the first floor. The hotel kitchen is very well[180] equipped, with fitted cupboards and the latest in catering equipment.[190] The hotel will be sold fully equipped and furnished, with[200] the exception of some personal furniture belonging to the present[210] owners. The outside of the building is in very good[220] condition, having been renovated only four years ago when the[230] present owners bought the property. Turnover has increased each year,[240] and the owners are very willing to show the figures[250] to a prospective purchaser. They are putting the hotel on[260] the market in order to buy a larger property. They[270] have one in mind which will become available next January,[280] so they are anxious to sell before then. If you[290] are interested in purchasing this property, we recommend you contact[300] us as soon as possible, because in our opinion there[310] is sure to be keen competition for it. Yours sincerely[320]

9 Preparing to sit an examination

revision ....

in the middle ....

protein ....

concentrate ....

When the time of year comes for examinations to start,[10] it is always a worrying time for students, their parents[20] and their teachers. Many clever, hard-working students do badly[30] in examinations because they become nervous. It is under these[40] conditions that carefully learned facts and well-prepared material can[50] be forgotten. How can such students be helped to pass[60] examinations? There is no doubt that thorough revision is important,[70] and this should start at least six weeks before the[80] examination date. Late-night revision should be avoided, particularly the[90] night before the examination, because increased mental activity before going[100] to bed interferes with restful sleep. Leave at least one[110] hour between studying and retiring. Learning to relax your body[120] also helps to relieve tension. A healthy diet will help[130] you to stay calm, so do make sure fresh fruit[140] and vegetables are included in it. On the morning of[150] the examination, breakfast should include egg, meat or fish for[160] protein, and not just toast and a cup of coffee.[170] In fact, it is better to drink milk or fruit[180] juice than tea or coffee. A good breakfast makes it[190] less likely that you will suddenly lose energy in the[200] middle of the morning. On the day before the examination,[210] aim to avoid last-minute worries by preparing all the[220] material needed for the following day such as rulers, pencils,[230] pens and calculators; and on the day itself, leave home[240] earlier than usual so that you can arrive at the[250] centre in good time and in a calm, relaxed state.[260] If you feel confused by an examination question, read it[270] through several times and jot down on a piece of[280] paper every thought that comes to mind. By doing this[290] you will be helping the mind to concentrate on the[300] question instead of allowing it to panic, and you should[310] soon find that all your fears and worries have disappeared.[320]

10 A letter to a student from his aunt

how much ....⌒......................   travellers' cheques ....⌒....

camera ....⌒...................

Dear Colin, Thank you for your letter to my family,[10] which we all read with interest. It is certainly good[20] news that you have succeeded in your first year at[30] university, and are now looking forward to the second year.[40] As your letter mentioned your plans to tour Europe during[50] your long summer vacation, I thought I would offer you[60] and your friends some advice on how to arrange your[70] holiday finances. Of course, the first thing to decide is[80] how much money you can afford to take. You will[90] then need to consider the best way to take it[100] with you, without the risk of losing it or breaking[110] any laws of the countries you will visit. The two[120] usual ways of taking money abroad are by purchasing travellers'[130] cheques or currency of the country of your destination. It[140] is wise to take a limited amount of currency in[150] order to get you through your first day or two.[160] It may come as a surprise to learn that there[170] are restrictions on the amount of currency that a person[180] can take into, or out of, certain countries. If you[190] decide to take travellers' cheques, you will have chosen the[200] most popular method of taking money abroad, and it is[210] important to note that this method is both safe and[220] simple to use. You will need to order these cheques[230] in advance of your leaving home. Some building societies offer[240] this service, but most people obtain their travellers' cheques from[250] their bank or travel agent. Follow the instructions which accompany[260] the travellers' cheques, and if you are unfortunate enough to[270] lose them or have them stolen they can be replaced[280] immediately. I do hope that you will have a most[290] enjoyable vacation and we all look forward to hearing about[300] your travels. Do remember to take your camera. Please give[310] our regards to your parents. With best wishes, Aunt Jane[320]

Section Fourteen
340-word passages

1 Green fingers

generally .... annoyance ....

Stonehenge .... apparently ....

murderer ....

It is a well-known fact that some people have[10] a way with plants. They have what is generally known[20] as 'green fingers', and it is a gift. If you[30] do not have it, there is no way you can[40] acquire it, however hard you try. I know what I[50] am talking about because my husband has green fingers and[60] I have not. This is a source of annoyance to[70] me, because I am very interested in gardening and know[80] a great deal more about plants than he does. Ask[90] me about almost any plant and I will tell you[100] its Latin name, how long it takes to flower, the[110] sort of soil it prefers, how much water it needs,[120] and so on. I will also tell you that any[130] plant on which I lay my hands has very little[140] chance of surviving the encounter. Last spring, working with great[150] care and strictly according to the book, I took some[160] cuttings from one of my favourite shrubs. I did everything[170] exactly right, even down to dipping the ends of the [180] cuttings into some hormone rooting powder before planting them in[190] the correct size of plant pot. As recommended, I put[200] one cutting in the middle of the pot and placed[210] another six in a circle round the rim. After eight[220] months they are still there, displaying as much life as[230] a matchstick model of Stonehenge. My dear partner, of course,[240] has no such problems. A few weeks ago he broke[250] off an apparently dead twig from the same shrub and[260] dropped it into a glass of water. Already it has[270] two new green shoots, and I would not be surprised[280] if it soon starts to flower while still in the[290] glass of water. It is small comfort to me that[300] I know the Latin name of the shrub. As far[310] as plants are concerned, I feel like a murderer and[320] I think you will agree that it is no comfort[330] to a murderer to know the name of his victim.[340]

2 An introduction to a gas-company brochure

appliances .... radiators ....

labour costs ....

Dear Customer, An important part of my job as sales[10] director for Regal Gas is making sure you get value[20] for money and are happy with the service we provide.[30] In the pages of this illustrated brochure you will find[40] some very special offers on a wide range of gas[50] appliances, and details of several services which we provide completely[60] free of charge. You will also find details of generous[70] trade-in offers on many appliances, including cookers and fires.[80] However, do not forget that these trade-in offers are[90] for a limited period only, so you will need to[100] act quickly if you wish to take advantage of them.[110] We have some real bargains in central heating, too. For[120] example, how would you like to have a boiler and[130] five radiators installed in your home for just one thousand[140] pounds, including labour costs! Many people, of course, believe that[150] there is nothing to match the glow of a beautiful[160] gas fire on a cold winter's day. We have dozens[170] of different fires available at very special prices, and we[180] are able to provide attractive credit facilities with repayment periods[190] of up to three years. Have you ever thought how[200] wonderful it would be to have a quick shower in[210] the morning before setting off for work or getting stuck[220] into those household tasks? Just turn to page five and[230] take your pick from the six showers illustrated there. Perhaps[240] your cooker is past its best or you would like[250] one with more features. If so, open this brochure at[260] the middle pages and you will be well on the[270] way to solving your problem. All our cookers can be[280] bought on easy terms, and we will take forty pounds[290] off the recommended retail price if you trade your existing[300] cooker in at the same time. Whatever your requirements, our[310] large team of expert fitters will ensure that installation is[320] carried out with as little inconvenience to you as possible.[330] Finally, remember that gas is still the most economical fuel.[340]

3 A letter to an agent from a mail-order company

replenished .... re-order ....

discontinued .... bikinis ....

urgently ....

Dear Mrs Barnet, Thank you for your letter of 10th[10] April regarding goods ordered by you on 14th March. According[20] to our records, the goods were despatched to you on[30] the 20th March and should have reached you by now.[40] We are chasing up the matter with the Post Office,[50] and no doubt they will be contacting you. The only[60] item which was not sent to you was the blue[70] jumper, catalogue number eighty-nine. This was out of stock[80] at the time we received your order, and we wrote[90] to you accordingly informing you of the situation. Our stocks[100] have now been replenished and, if you still require the[110] jumper, you should reorder using the pink order form enclosed.[120] Whilst writing we would draw your attention to special offers[130] from our winter catalogue. Many items of ladies' and children's[140] clothing have been reduced, some to below half price. Discontinued[150] lines of bedding have also been drastically reduced. Our new[160] summer catalogue is now ready for despatch and should be[170] with you shortly. We feel sure you will be pleasantly[180] surprised at the summer-season clothes in this catalogue. We[190] are fortunate in having stylish clothes designed by Jean Redmond[200] in our collection. Her designs are original, and she uses[210] bright colours and floral prints for skirts, blouses and dresses.[220] We are also able to boast the best collection of[230] swimwear ever seen in a mail-order catalogue. You can[240] choose from over one hundred one-piece swimsuits and bikinis[250] which cater for sizes eight to eighteen. We are sure[260] you and your clients will find something to your liking,[270] and we look forward to receiving your orders shortly. Remember[280] that you can now telephone your order through to us.[290] This is particularly useful when goods are required urgently, as[300] we can guarantee delivery within forty-eight hours of receiving[310] your order. Our lines are open from eight-thirty a.m.[320] to five-thirty p.m. Monday to Saturday, and nine-thirty[330] a.m. to twelve noon on Sundays. Yours sincerely, John Matthews[340]

4 Hayfever

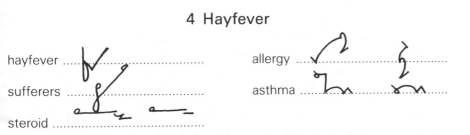

hayfever ....

sufferers ....

steroid ....

allergy ....

asthma ....

Throughout the months of June and July, it is estimated[10] that some five million people suffer from hayfever in this[20] country. The most common symptoms are sneezing, a blocked nose[30] and itching eyes. Some people suffer from only the occasional[40] bout of sneezing, but others find that they can barely[50] see through bloodshot eyes for up to two months. There[60] is no real cure for hayfever, but it is not[70] a really dangerous condition. However, the allergy can cause much[80] inconvenience. For instance, it can prevent youngsters from joining in[90] summer sporting activities at school, and it can have a[100] detrimental effect on those unfortunate sufferers who are about to[110] sit examinations. The main culprit in causing the allergy is[120] pollen from grass, trees and flowers. During the hayfever season[130] the Asthma Research Council gives out a daily reading of[140] the pollen count. The day's pollen count is the average[150] number of grass pollen grains to occupy a cubic metre[160] of air throughout a twenty-four-hour period. It is[170] known that the pollen count needs to reach fifty before[180] most sufferers will have any reaction. When the pollen count[190] is as high as six hundred, some people can suffer[200] the symptoms of asthma. However, three hundred is the count[210] which is considered to cause problems for most people. The[220] highest count recorded in London was in nineteen eighty-four[230] when the reading was eight hundred and forty. As with[240] all allergies, the best way to treat hayfever is to[250] avoid its cause. This, of course, is much easier said[260] than done, as it is nearly impossible to avoid contact[270] with pollen. Even in the cities and alongside the uncut[280] grass verges of motorways, the pollen count can be high.[290] It would seem that we cannot be saved from contact[300] with it even inside a motor car. One treatment for[310] hayfever which is considered to be effective is steroid drugs.[320] These are available in the form of a nasal spray[330] and have been shown to cause no harmful side-effects.[340]

5 A letter about a language conference

most pleased ....⟨outline⟩.......   graduates ....⟨outline⟩.......

few words ....⟨outline⟩.......

Dear Sir, Thank you for your letter inviting me to[10] the language conference to be held on 4th April. I[20] shall be most pleased to attend. Concerning the request for[30] me to give a talk on English as a second[40] language, I am happy to say that I can oblige.[50] However, you have given no indication as to the amount[60] of time which would be allocated to the speech. May[70] I suggest that twenty to thirty minutes would be long[80] enough to give a brief outline and, at the same[90] time, short enough to ensure that the audience does not[100] become bored. As there will be a number of new[110] graduates in the audience, I would like to say a[120] few words regarding career prospects in the area of language[130] teaching. For instance, those with relevant degrees may well be[140] interested in spending a few years working abroad. There are[150] many opportunities for such graduates all over the world in[160] the field of teaching English as a second language. Wide[170] and varied experience can be gained in this way. Well-[180] qualified teachers of English are much in demand and career[190] prospects are very bright indeed. I feel it would help[200] me to give a more interesting talk if I had[210] the use of an overhead projector and also, if possible,[220] a video recorder. If you are unable to provide the[230] latter, please would you let me know so that I[240] can make the appropriate amendments to my prepared notes. With²⁵⁰ regard to accommodation requirements, I shall need a single room²⁶⁰ for the evening prior to the day of the conference.²⁷⁰ I would be grateful if your secretary could make the²⁸⁰ necessary arrangements for me. Thank you for extending the invitation²⁹⁰ to my wife. Unfortunately, she is attending a training course³⁰⁰ which clashes with the date of the conference, so will³¹⁰ be unable to attend. I look forward to attending the³²⁰ conference, and will be most interested to hear the views³³⁰ and opinions of all the speakers. Yours faithfully, John Forsyth³⁴⁰

6 Details of weekend breaks offered by a hotel group

charge ....   babies ....

(babes ....)

You will find our hotels all over the country. Some¹⁰ are in cities, some are in glorious country settings, some²⁰ are by the sea. The smallest one has just four³⁰ bedrooms and the largest has over ninety. The bedrooms have⁴⁰ all recently been modernized and tastefully decorated, and each one⁵⁰ has its own bathroom, colour television and telephone. We provide⁶⁰ a tea and coffee tray so you can make a⁷⁰ hot drink at any time. A morning newspaper is brought⁸⁰ to your room and is included in the price. A⁹⁰ weekend break at one of these hotels is wonderful value¹⁰⁰ for money. It will cost you only twenty pounds per¹¹⁰ person per night plus VAT, and will include a traditional¹²⁰ English breakfast. You can take your break between Thursday and¹³⁰ Sunday, the minimum stay being two nights. At some hotels¹⁴⁰ you can also enjoy a mid-week break at the¹⁵⁰ same price. If you would like to have dinner at¹⁶⁰ the hotel, we are sure you will be attracted by¹⁷⁰ another special offer. You can enjoy a meal that really¹⁸⁰ costs ten pounds for only seven pounds – a considerable saving.¹⁹⁰ You can book this in advance or on arrival at²⁰⁰ the hotel, for as many nights of your stay as²¹⁰ you wish. If you would like to bring your children²²⁰ with you, they will be made very welcome. There is²³⁰ no charge at all for babies aged two and under.²⁴⁰ Cots are available free of charge. Children aged between three²⁵⁰ and twelve can share your room for only five pounds²⁶⁰ each, including breakfast. If you wish them to have their²⁷⁰ own room, they will be charged at seventy per cent²⁸⁰ of the full weekend price. Get away from shopping and²⁹⁰ gardening and treat yourself and your family to a wonderful³⁰⁰ weekend. Do you prefer hills, lakes, rivers, forests, the beach,³¹⁰ villages, towns or cities? Look through the brochure and select³²⁰ the hotel of your choice.

Telephone the hotel to confirm[330] that your dates are available before completing the booking form.[340]

7 Dealing with incoming office mail

remittance   enclosures

recipient   charities

Methods of dealing with incoming mail will of course vary[10] from office to office, but whatever method is used certain[20] principles must apply. There should be definite guidelines laid down[30] for staff to follow. On its arrival, the mail should[40] be sorted and any letters marked private or confidential should[50] be put on one side for direct delivery to the[60] persons concerned. Usually the date is stamped on the outside[70] of these envelopes, so that the recipients can see when[80] they arrived. The rest of the mail is then opened,[90] and great care must be taken to remove the total[100] contents from the envelopes. In large companies a letter-opening[110] machine may be used which slices off a tiny portion[120] of the envelope, but small offices will probably use a[130] paper-knife. Enclosures should be fastened to the letter at[140] once, if this has not been done before despatch. Then[150] the letters are date stamped. Any remittances should be entered[160] in a remittance register and if any enclosures have been[170] omitted, a note to this effect should be attached to[180] the letter. If a document needs to be seen by[190] several people, one of two methods may be followed. It[200] can either be photocopied and a separate copy sent to[210] each person, or a circulation slip giving the names of[220] the people to receive it may be attached to the[230] original. When the first recipient has read it, he or[240] she initials the slip and passes the document and the[250] slip to the next person on the list, and so[260] on. It is important to indicate at the end of[270] the list the name of the person to whom the[280] document should be returned when all concerned have seen it.[290] Often it is the practice for offices to keep envelopes[300] for several days, in case there is any query over[310] the date of delivery or the omission of an enclosure.[320] Many people remove postage stamps to donate to charities, who[330] can raise much-needed money by selling them to collectors.[340]

8 The work of a voluntary secretary

correspondence   bed-sitter

reproducing   time-consuming

At some time or other you may be asked to[10] undertake some form of voluntary work. Organizations are always looking[20] for people willing to act as secretaries, treasurers, or fund-[30] raisers, as well as those willing to do practical work.[40] Perhaps the most exciting of these posts is that of[50] the voluntary secretary, and it is important to consider carefully[60] what is involved before agreeing to take on such a[70] commitment. Whatever kind of organization it is, correspondence will arrive[80] frequently and will have to be dealt with promptly and[90] efficiently. You will need a typewriter and, of course, the[100] skill to use it. Copies of all correspondence will have[110] to be kept for the records and filed regularly, so[120] you will need to be a methodical worker. You will[130] also require space to keep the files, minute books and[140] other such records which accumulate in any organization. So if[150] you live in a tiny bed-sitter, the position of[160] secretary may not be for you. Other duties may include[170] calling committee meetings, and this often involves finding suitable accommodation[180] for them. Minutes of the last meeting are usually circulated[190] with the notice of the next meeting, so that committee[200] members may study them to ensure their accuracy and check[210] that any actions decided upon at the last meeting have[220] been carried out. The secretary takes the minutes of the[230] meeting and needs to have facilities for reproducing them. Voluntary[240] organizations often use an ink duplicator as it is the[250] cheapest method of producing a large number of copies but,[260] if your organization is not too big, a photocopier may[270] be used. Your local library may provide this facility; alternatively,[280] you may find a small local business such as a[290] travel agent who will make copies for you while you[300] wait. You will need to buy stamps and keep records[310] of all your expenditure on postage and telephones. Being a[320] voluntary secretary can be very time-consuming. You should therefore[330] think carefully before you agree to take on the job.[340]

9 Reminiscences of childhood

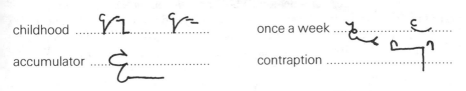

childhood ....   once a week ....

accumulator ....   contraption ....

Sometimes, when I switch on an electric light, I think[10] back to my childhood and wonder how we managed without[20] electricity. When we first moved to the country before the[30] start of the First World War, we lived in a[40] cottage which had no electricity, gas, running water or drainage[50] facilities, yet my parents managed to bring up three children[60] without complaining about what a hard life it was. For[70] us children, of course, it was great fun. Water was[80] obtained by dipping a bucket into a well at the[90] end of the garden. It was lovely clear water. We[100] always boiled it before drinking it or using it for[110] cooking. For lighting we used an oil lamp which, unless[120] it was adjusted very frequently, sent a column of black[130] smoke up to the ceiling. When we went upstairs we[140] had to carry candles to light the way and, of[150] course, we had to be very careful not to set[160] anything alight. The least said about toilet facilities the better.[170] We did our bathing once a week in a tin[180] tub in front of the log fire, and no water[190] was thrown away until every member of the family had[200] had his or her turn. We had a primitive radio[210] which was powered by a large accumulator, and my brothers[220] and I had to carry this heavy contraption a mile[230] to have it recharged when it ran down. Naturally, we[240] did not waste the electricity by keeping the radio on[250] for long. This was before the advent of television, of[260] course, so we used to provide our own entertainment by[270] playing board games such as snakes and ladders, draughts and[280] chess. Looking back on those days, I am amazed at[290] how much the living standards of most people in this[300] country have risen over the past sixty years or so.[310] I am also amazed that in spite of all the[320] inconveniences, I thoroughly enjoyed my childhood, and I would certainly[330] not have wished to change places with any other child.[340]

10 A special offer of a book on European birds

European ...... 𝑦 ....

indexed .... 4̵ ....

compiled .... " ☞ ....

instalments .... ƫ ᷁ ....

Dear Member, We thank you for your cheque for sixteen[10] pounds, which renews your membership of the European Bird Society[20] for a further twelve months. You may be aware that[30] this year the Society celebrates its tenth birthday, and to[40] mark this occasion we are pleased to be able to[50] offer you the opportunity of buying a book on European[60] birds at a greatly reduced price. The book will be[70] on sale in book shops from the 1st of next[80] month for the sum of eighteen pounds but, if you[90] reserve your copy with us before the end of this[100] month, you will be entitled to buy it for only[110] thirteen pounds, thus saving yourself five pounds. We believe it[120] is a book that every member of the Society will[130] wish to have on their book shelves. It is not[140] only a valuable reference book, but is full of interesting[150] facts about the environment in which the birds live, the[160] food they cat, their nest-building habits and their distribution[170] throughout Europe. The book is indexed in such a way[180] that you can study the life of one particular bird,[190] or the country in which it lives or the food[200] which it eats. If you are travelling through Europe on[210] holiday then it is, in our opinion, an excellent companion[220] for the journey, as it will teach you all you[230] want to know about the many different birds you will[240] see. The material in the book has been compiled over[250] many years, and has been written so that even young[260] children can understand it and gain pleasure from its contents.[270] There are illustrations of each kind of bird and all[280] the drawings and photographs are in colour. If you wish[290] to reserve your copy, please complete the form attached and[300] post it today in the pre-paid envelope. If you[310] wish to pay for the book in instalments, you may[320] do so at no extra cost. We very much hope[330] you will take advantage of this special offer. Yours truly[340]

Section Fifteen
360-word passages

1 A letter about property repairs

underfelt .....(shorthand symbol).....................   woodworm .....(shorthand symbol).........

infestation .....(shorthand symbol)......(shorthand symbol).....   replastering .....(shorthand symbol).....

Dear Mr Evans, Further to our recent meeting at your[10] property last Monday, I set out below a list of[20] essential works required to the property. The roof covering has[30] a very limited life and should be replaced using underfelt[40] with asbestos tiles laid on top; any rotten battens should[50] be replaced at the same time. It is advisable to[60] remove chimney stacks which are not being used and to[70] repoint those in use. The rendering to the rear is[80] hollow in places and should be hacked off and replaced.[90] Existing gutters are of cast iron. These are defective in[100] places and should be replaced by plastic gutters. External joinery[110] appeared in good order, but a coat of paint would[120] help to preserve its life. Woodworm attack was noticed to[130] many internal fittings, particularly the staircase. It is recommended that[140] the staircase be treated with a suitable chemical solution to[150] destroy the woodworm and prevent any further infestation. High damp-[160] meter readings were obtained throughout the ground floor. The plaster[170] will have to be removed up to three metres high[180] in all the ground floor walls, and a damp-proof[190] course injected before replastering can begin. Plumbing and sanitary fittings[200] are in need of complete removal, replacing any lead piping[210] with copper tubing. In particular, the facilities in the bathroom[220] are old-fashioned. A new suite with a low-level[230] water closet should be installed. Ceilings to the front and[240] rear bedrooms are badly cracked. These should be recovered with[250] plasterboard and finished with an attractive artex design. The property[260] needs to be rewired as the original rubber wiring is[270] in a very dangerous condition. In order to comply with[280] the safety regulations laid down by the Electricity Board, it[290] will have to be replaced with plastic-coated wire. The[300] total cost of these essential repairs will be four thousand,[310] three hundred pounds, plus Value Added Tax at the standard[320] rate. Many other repairs could be undertaken to improve the[330] property, such as building an attractive feature fireplace in the[340] lounge. Please let us know if we can be of[350] any further assistance. Yours sincerely, Johnson and Grant Building Contractors[360]

2 Rules for safety at the seaside

lifeguard ....

lifeboat ....

helicopter ....

hazards ....

cramp ....

Most people like to spend time on the beach, and[10] a summer holiday at the seaside can be very enjoyable[20] and relaxing. It is vital, however, that the sea is[30] treated with respect because a day that started out as[40] a pleasant occasion can end in an accident. People who[50] live in towns and cities are often not aware of[60] the dangers of the coast, and they are the ones[70] who are probably most at risk. It is essential to[80] apply common sense, and to adopt a few basic rules[90] of safety if accidents are to be avoided. The arrangements[100] for life-saving vary widely from place to place. A[110] swimmer in trouble may find himself being rescued by a[120] fully trained lifeguard or by a large lifeboat with a[130] crew of seven or eight, or even by a helicopter.[140] On the other hand, many beaches have no rescue facilities[150] at all, so always find out what arrangements are[160] on the beach you are using. Look out for notices[170] which tell you of any special problems, and get advice[180] about any local hazards from lifeguards, fishermen or residents. If[190] the safe-bathing area is marked by flags, then make[200] sure you only swim in the area between the flags.[210] Never swim if the red flags are flying, as this[220] means it is unsafe. Do not swim on your own,[230] but always stay near other people. When you get into[240] the water, swim parallel to the beach rather than out[250] to sea. This will reduce the risk of getting out[260] of your depth, and not being able to stand if[270] you get cramp or need a rest from swimming. It[280] is amazing how many parents allow their children to get[290] into difficulties. Very young children should be supervised all the[300] time, even if they can swim quite well. If they[310] are going in to paddle, an adult should walk through[320] the water first to make sure the sea bed is[330] level. Toys like boats and rubber rings should only be[340] used when the tide is coming in, and should have[350] a line attached to them for an adult to hold.[360]

3 A letter about a property for sale

oil-fired ....

utility ....

studios ....

conservatory ....

Dear Mr Black, Further to your visit to our office[10] last week, we are sending you details of an excellent[20] property which we think will be of interest to you.[30] It consists of a large three-storey house and a[40] separate outbuilding. It is set in half an acre of[50] land. There are well-stocked, mature gardens to the front[60] and rear. The property itself has been well maintained and[70] is in excellent decorative order throughout. In fact, viewing is[80] essential to appreciate fully the internal improvements which have been[90] carried out. Oil-fired central heating has been installed and[100] there is a radiator in every room. The house has[110] been recently rewired and the loft is fully insulated. The[120] windows and external doors are double-glazed. All carpets, curtains[130] and fittings are to be included in the final sale[140] price. The ground floor consists of a large and impressive[150] hallway, four reception rooms, a utility room and a modern[160] well-equipped kitchen. The first floor comprises five very large[170] bedrooms, all with fitted wardrobes of the finest quality. There[180] are two bathrooms on this floor, each with a coloured[190] suite, low-level water closet and shower unit. The third[200] floor comprises two extremely large rooms with windows to all[210] sides. These rooms would be ideal for use as studios,[220] because of the amount of natural light which can enter.[230] The outbuilding mentioned earlier would be ideal for use as[240] a garage, and is capable of housing up to four[250] cars. A very large conservatory and a patio have been[260] built to the rear of the house. We strongly recommend[270] viewing of this property in order to appreciate fully its[280] many attractions. In the meantime, please find enclosed a set[290] of photographs which depict some of the finer features of[300] the property. Please do not hesitate to contact me to[310] arrange a convenient time for viewing. I am in the[320] office between nine and ten o'clock each morning. However, if[330] you are unable to make contact during these hours, my[340] secretary will be available to assist you. I look forward[350] to hearing from you in the near future. Yours sincerely[360]

4 A letter of instruction from a manager to his secretary

progression .... top drawer ...

names and addresses ... presentation ...

Dear Ann, I shall not be in the office at[10] all next week as I shall be attending the sales[20] convention which is to be held in London. However, arrangements[30] are still to be made regarding Jean Smith's retirement. As[40] you know, Jean has been with the company for some[50] thirty years.

She started work as the office junior and[60] made steady progress up the ladder of promotion. Jean worked[70] in many departments before deciding her future lay in the[80] area of accountancy. By spending several years attending night classes[90] at a local college, she gained the requisite qualifications to[100] commence working as a junior accountant. From that time on[110] she succeeded in gaining several promotions, until she finally became[120] chief accountant to the company. Would you please draft a[130] history of Jean's working life with the company, commencing with[140] her humble beginnings as office junior? If you search through[150] the records in the personnel department, you will find details[160] of her career progression together with the relevant dates. In[170] the top drawer of my desk you will find the[180] names and addresses of the people with whom Jean worked[190] closely. Please would you contact these people and ask if[200] they could attend the celebration evening we are arranging for[210] Jean? If necessary, arrange for transport so they can be[220] collected from their homes and taken to the Grand Hotel[230] where the celebration is being held on Tuesday, 9th August[240] at seven o'clock. Donations made by staff members towards the[250] retirement present have been most generous. The total now has[260] reached two hundred and twenty-five pounds. It is felt[270] by all concerned that the presentation gift should be a[280] lead-crystal table lamp. Apparently, Jean has been admiring one[290] which is on display in Harrison's window. Will you collect[300] a cheque from Mr Brown for the required amount and[310] purchase the lamp tomorrow morning. While you are out, call[320] into the offices of the taxi firm we normally use,[330] and order a taxi to collect Jean from her home[340] at six-thirty on the Tuesday evening. Following that, go[350]to the florists and order thirty roses for Jean. Thanks.[360]

5 A letter about house and contents insurance

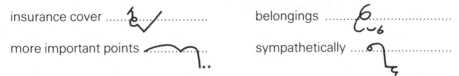

Dear Mr Hunt, Do you know how much your house[10] contents are insured for? If you are not sure, or[20] if you have not made a complete valuation of your[30] contents at today's prices, the chances are that your insurance[40] cover is not high enough. It is also possible that[50] you do not fully understand the terms of your cover.[60] Some policies are not at all easy to read. People[70] often make a claim and then discover they are not[80] covered in the way they thought they were. This can[90] result in a reduced claim. This is why we are[100] writing to tell you about our new policy. It will[110] cover your home and your belongings and will take care[120] of all your worries. If you would like to know[130] more, just ring the number at the top of this[140] letter. The call is completely free. We shall be pleased[150] to tell you about our scheme, and if you like[160] what you hear, you can take out a policy straight[170] away. You will be covered from that moment. Alternatively, you[180] can just complete the simple form enclosed with this letter,[190] and post it to us in the reply-paid envelope.[200] In the meantime, we should like to tell you about[210] some of the more important points that make our policy[220] different from all the others. There is no need to[230] make an exact valuation of all your contents. As long[240] as the total value does not exceed twenty-five thousand[250] pounds, you do not have to provide a detailed list[260] of every item in your home. If you should be[270] involved in any kind of dispute, say with a neighbour[280] or a shop, we will provide free advice and legal[290] expenses. Items which are often subject to a separate charge[300] are included in our policy at no extra charge. Some[310] examples of these are your television set, video equipment and[320] freezer. We are also proud of the fact that if[330] you need to make a claim, it will be dealt[340] with sympathetically and, above all, quickly. Why not take this[350] opportunity to start afresh with a new policy. Yours sincerely[360]

6 The advantages of cycling

slowly .... *C*........................   upright .... *y* .... *y* ....

more and more people .... *C*

Cycling is not only a very good way of keeping[10] fit: it can also be fun. It is faster than[20] walking and it is free. You can cycle as quickly[30] or as slowly as you like. There is no need[40] to speed along as if you are in one of[50] the major national cycling races. Your bike can be the[60] latest sports model or it can be the old-fashioned[70] upright kind. Folding bikes are very useful for people who[80] want to take them in the boot of a car.[90] It is a great idea to take a bike with[100] you when you go on holiday. You will see places[110] and sights you would never notice if you were driving[120] around in a car. Apart from increasing the strength of[130] your legs, cycling is an excellent way to build up[140] your heart and lungs, provided you push hard enough for[150] long enough. It can be better than jogging as you[160] do not have to put all your weight on your[170] feet. For this reason it is much easier for anyone[180] with painful feet. If you live within a few miles[190] of your work, why not try going by bike? You[200] will be surprised how quickly you can get there. It[210] is often possible to be faster than other forms of[220] transport and, of course, you can save money on bus[230] and train fares. Even when travelling by train, you may[240] be able to take a bike with you. On most[250] routes, you can put it in the guard's van at[260] no cost. Try shopping by bike. If you attach a[270] basket to the bike, quite large amounts of shopping can[280] be carried with surprising ease. Cycling in the country is,[290] of course, absolute pleasure. The lanes are quiet, and you[300] can breathe the clean air and can listen to the[310] birds singing. Just beware of cars that seem to appear[320] from nowhere. Keep to the side of the road, and [330] stay in single file on busy or narrow roads. More[340] and more people are discovering the pleasures of cycling. Why[350] not join your local cycling club and make new friends.[360]

7 A company chairman's address

morale ....

(moral ....)

financial statement ....

balance sheet ....

bonus shares ....

preferential ....

Ladies and Gentlemen, This is the fortieth annual general meeting[10] of our company, and I am very pleased to be[20] able to tell you that our profits for last year[30] were the highest ever recorded. I feel sure you will[40] wish to join with me in expressing thanks and appreciation[50] to all those employees who have made this situation possible.[60] Our staff are loyal to the company and work very[70] hard. Morale is excellent and we have no problems in[80] keeping staff, as we endeavour to make their conditions of[90] employment as good as we can. Last year you approved[100] the election of a member of the works committee to[110] the Board of Directors. This proved to be a very[120] valuable move. I would like to convey my thanks to[130] this staff representative, Mr James Green, and to say that[140] I hope he will continue to serve on the Board[150] for many years to come. As you may be aware,[160] we have just modernized our office accommodation and installed some[170] of the best electronic equipment available. This should help to[180] make our company even more efficient, once staff have been[190] trained to use the new machines. Our new assembly plant[200] in Newport is nearing completion, and it is expected to[210] come into commission by the end of the year and[220] reach peak output some six months later. We have managed[230] to keep our prices steady over the year, despite rises[240] in the rate of inflation. Where increases have been necessary[250] because of the rise in raw-material prices, we have[260] restricted them in an effort to retain all our existing[270] customers. The financial statement and balance sheet are before you[280] for approval, and I feel sure you will support our[290] recommendations. The proposal to issue bonus shares at a rate[300] of two for one should meet with your approval, as[310] should the proposal to offer shares to workers at preferential[320] prices. It is difficult to forecast what the future holds[330] for the company, but I remain confident that we shall[340] be able to cope with any further increases in costs[350] and that we shall continue to enjoy very considerable success.[360]

8 A letter about a natural history society

radius ....   excursions ....

observatory ....   purposely ....

surplus ....

Dear Mr Watson, Thank you very much for your letter[10] received today regarding membership of our Natural History Society. We[20] should be very pleased to welcome you and, as you[30] say, it will be a good way of getting to[40] know people with similar interests to yours. I note that[50] you have only just moved into the neighbourhood. Our indoor[60] meetings are held at the Community Centre on Monday evenings[70] from September to April, commencing at seven-thirty. We have[80] speakers on a variety of interesting topics, and they often[90] have excellent photographs or films to accompany their talks. Coffee[100] is served afterwards and the whole evening is a very[110] pleasant social occasion. Throughout the year we have outdoor activities,[120] sometimes at weekends and sometimes in the evenings, so that[130] everyone has the opportunity to take part in at least[140] some of them. We visit varied habitats within a radius[150] of about fifty miles. As well as this, we have[160] two weekends away each year, one in the autumn and[170] one in the spring. Usually about a dozen people go[180] on these very enjoyable excursions, which give us the opportunity[190] to visit places that are too far away for a [200] day trip. The Society arranges accommodation either at an observatory[210] or in bed-and-breakfast establishments. The cost is not[220] high, and is sometimes subsidized from the Society's funds. We[230] have a library of natural-history books which can be[240] borrowed completely free of charge for periods of up to[250] three weeks. Our membership fee is purposely kept low so[260] that people with limited means are able to join the[270] Society, and we run several money-raising events during the[280] year to make this possible. These are hard work, but[290] all who take part enjoy the experience and find it[300] rewarding. Surplus funds are donated to national or local appeals[310] for conservation. Each month we produce a bulletin giving information[320] on forthcoming events, reports of meetings, and members' records. I[330] enclose some past issues for you to see what we[340] do. I hope you will be convinced that we offer[350] the kind of social life you are seeking. Yours sincerely[360]

9 The hazards of bidding at an auction

auction .... ⌢⌢ ....   protracted ..... ┼⌐‾ ....

accidental ...... X ....   inexperienced ...... ⅄/⌐ ....

A friend of mine attended an auction sale recently, and[10] was delighted when she successfully bid for and bought a[20] Welsh dresser. She was especially pleased because she said the[30] bidding had been keen and she had competition for the[40] item from several people at the front of the room.[50] Of course, I was pleased for her success, but as[60] I work in an auction room I thought she should[70] know about the rules relating to an auction sale in[80] case she made an expensive mistake on another occasion. Present-[90]day auction sales have changed little since A.D. one hundred[100] and ninety-three when the Roman Empire was to be[110] sold by public auction to the highest bidder. If you[120] are going to attend a sale of goods or property[130] by public auction, it is important to realize that a[140] successful bid means an immediate and binding contract between the[150] parties concerned. This method of selling has its advantages because[160] it eliminates the delays and disappointments of a protracted deal,[170] or one that falls through because of a higher bid.[180] There are also disadvantages, however, and it is very important[190] to be aware that once the auctioneer's hammer has fallen,[200] the bid is binding. A moment of poor concentration or[210] an accidental movement of the hand or head can mean[220] you are the owner of an item you do not[230] want. This rule is many centuries old. A contract is[240] made when the final bid is accepted, and the buyer[250] has just twenty-eight days to complete the transaction. If[260] he is unable to complete in time, the vendors of[270] the item can ask for another auction to be held,[280] but the bidder who could not complete the purchase will[290] be responsible for the costs of the second auction. Anyone[300] who is proposing to attend such a sale should make[310] sure of two important facts, firstly that he has adequate[320] funds to meet the cost of the item, and secondly,[330] that he is certain of the true value of the[340] item of interest. Quite clearly, an auction room can be[350] a place full of potential hazards for the inexperienced bidder.[360]

10 Notice of a conference and a proposed merger

freezers ....⟋........................ shareholders ...⟋⟍...............

redundancies ....⟋⌒⟍ 6...............

On Friday, 18th August, this company will be holding its[10] annual conference and dinner dance. All staff are invited to[20] attend the conference which begins at ten a.m. in the[30] Devon Suite of the George Hotel, and is followed by[40] the dinner dance in the hotel beginning at seven p.m.[50] The main topic of the conference this year will be[60] the expansion of the company. As you may already be[70] aware, we have been trading for some years with Jones[80] Brothers, and your Board of Directors and that of Jones[90] Brothers are of the opinion that the companies would benefit[100] from a merger. Such a merger would mean we were[110] able to offer a more comprehensive service to our customers[120] because we have a greater skill in the manufacture of[130] small electrical household goods, whilst Jones Brothers have experience with[140] larger electrical goods such as washing-machines, cookers and freezers.[150] Accordingly, we have put forward a bid of three million,[160] four hundred thousand pounds for Jones Brothers and are awaiting[170] the comments of their accountants and shareholders. If this merger[180] goes ahead, it is estimated there will be an immediate[190] need for an extra fifty employees, and by the end[200] of next year this figure will increase to eighty new[210] employees. Jones Brothers are holding their own conference next month,[220] at which the proposed merger with our company will be[230] discussed. Your Board will report back to you on the[240] outcome of those discussions, but we look forward to your[250] comments on the occasion of our conference on the 18th.[260] Please note that tickets for the dinner dance will cost[270] twenty pounds each and are available from the personnel department.[280] During the evening there will be the usual prize-giving[290] ceremony, and this year we are fortunate in that Lord[300] and Lady Trent have agreed to be guests of honour[310] and will of course present the prizes. Please do try[320] to attend this important annual event. Your opinions and questions[330] about the proposed merger will be welcomed, and your Board[340] wishes to reassure you that this would not cause any[350] redundancies among our own workforce. With my best wishes, Chairman[360]

Alphabetical list of outlines

above address ....

above all ....

absolutely ....

access ....

accidental ....

accordingly ....

accountant ....

accumulator ....

achievement ....

acknowledgement ....

action-packed ....

activities ....

additional expenses ....

administered ....

advertising agency ....

agreed ....

agreement ....

allergy ....

alongside ....

alternative ....

amalgamating ....

amazing ....

ambulance ....

amusing ....

anchor ....

anniversary ....

annoyance ....

answer ....

ante-room ....

anxious ....

apologize ....

apparently ....

appliances ....

applicants ....

application ....

appointment ....

appreciated ....

appropriate ....

approximately

aptitude

arrangement

art-work

as far as

as soon as

as soon as possible

as well as

assemble

assessor

assistance

assistant chef

association

asthma

at present

at the end of the day

at the present time

at the same time

auction

audio-typing

Australia

automatically

babes

babies

background

badly

balanced

balance sheet

basic

Baxter

bed-sitter

beefburger

bee-keeping

belongings

bicycle

bidet

bikinis

blemished

blood pressure

boardroom

bonus shares

bookkeeper

booklet

branches

breakfast

brewed

brochures

bungalows

burglary

bus service

business letter

camera

candidates

card

career

castle

catalogue number

caterers

celebrate

centralized

certainly

certificates

chairperson

charge

charities

chemicals

chemists

childhood

children

chop-suey

Christmas

circular

citizens

clarify

clearly

comfortable

comforting

commercial

communicate

companies

compensation

competence

compiled

complain

comprehensive

computer

computer system

concentrate

cones

conference facilities

confidential

conjunction

consequently

conservatory

consisted

contest

continuing

contraption

contributions

conventional

co-operation

cordially

correspondence

costly

countryside

coupled

course of action

courteous

cramp

credit

credit card

crown

currency

current account

currently

dandelion

dating

days of the week

Dear Sir or Madam

debit balance

decision

delicious

delivery date

demonstrated

departmental

department stores

deplorable

deposit account

depriving

destination

developer

development

diary

dieting

diplomacy

disadvantages

disappointment

discontinued

discounted

discussion

display

dissatisfied

donation

double-glazed

dozens

drastically

draw your attention

earrings

economic

economical

edition

effectiveness

electronic

eligible

emblem

emergency

emigrated

emphasis

employers

enclosures

encounter

encouragement

end-product

engaged

engineer

enrolment

en-suite

enthusiasm

environment

envisage

errors

escaped

especially

essential

established

European

exactly

excellent

exception

excessive

exchange ....

excursions ....

exorbitant ....

exotic ....

expenditure ....

extension ....

extra ....

facilities ....

fast-food ....

favourably ....

feasibility ....

features ....

fee ....

few words ....

filmed ....

financial statement ....

fireman ....

first class ....

first of all ....

first thing in the
    morning ....

foreman ....

forgetful ....

forthcoming ....

for the attention ....

free of charge ....

freephone ....

freepost ....

freezers ....

frequently ....

Friday evening ....

Friday night ....

friendships ....

from the beginning ....

generally ....

get away ....

glorious ....

glossy ....

good enough ....

gradually ....

graduates ....

grandparents ....

grateful ....

great care ....

great-grandparents ....

great importance ....

great interest ....

greatly ....

greenhouse ....

groomed ....

gymnastics ....

habitat ....

hand-made ....

handrail ....

hand-spun ....

happily ....

hard day's work ....

hayfever ....

hazards ....

helicopter ....

he or she ....

herewith ....

highway ....

hours of work ....

housekeeping ....

how much ....

hundreds of ....

husband ....

I am pleased ....

I am writing ....

I was pleased ....

illusions ....

illustrations ....

imagination ....

impression ....

in addition ....

in full agreement ....

in order to be ....

in such a way ....

in the meantime ....

in the middle ....

in the morning ....

in the past ....

in your letter ....

inception ....

incident ....

inclusion ....

income tax ....

inconvenience ....

incorrectly ....

indexed ....

indexing ....

individually ....

industrial action ....

inevitable ....

inevitably ....

inexpensive ....

inexperienced ....

infestation ....

inflation ....

influence ....

informed ....

infringe ....

ingredients ....

inserted ....

inspect ....

installed ....

instalments ....

instruction ....

insufficient ....

insurance ....

insurance company ....

insurance cover ....

insurance policy ....

integral ....

interested ....

interest-free ....

interest rate ....

intermediate ....

international ....

interrupted ....

interview ....

introductory ....

investigate ....

invitation ....

invoice ....

it goes without saying ....

it is likely ....

it is necessary ....

January ....

Jennifer ....

June ....

kindest

kindly

labour costs

landlord

language

last Friday

last summer

late

laundry

leaflet

library

lifeboat

lifeguard

light

likely

literature

livelihood

luckily

luxury

magnificent

mail order

maintenance

managing director

manufacturers

manuscripts

Margaret

maximum

Mediterranean

member of staff

membership

mentioned

menus

merchandise

merchants

methodically

misfire

moisturize

Monday morning

monthly

moral

morale

more and more people

more important points

mortgage

most pleased.............

murderer.............

mutually.............

names and addresses.............

nationally.............

necessary.............

necessity.............

newspaper.............

next-door neighbour.............

next Friday.............

no point.............

no reply.............

noisier.............

observatory.............

obstacle race.............

obviously.............

off-peak.............

offset.............

oil-fired.............

old-established.............

old-fashioned.............

omit.............

once a week.............

ophthalmics.............

optician.............

orange.............

orders.............

ordinary.............

organization.............

organized.............

ornate.............

outnumbered.............

outweigh.............

overcharged.............

overcome.............

overdrawn.............

over-exposure.............

overhanging.............

overhead projector.............

overnight.............

paperweight.............

paperwork.............

paragraphs.............

particular .....

partnership .....

part-time .....

passenger seat .....

perform .....

performance .....

period .....

permanent .....

personal .....

personal possessions .....

personal telephone

   service .....

personality .....

personally .....

perspective .....

persuade .....

petition .....

photocopier .....

photocopying .....

picnics .....

picturesque .....

pineapple .....

pizza .....

pleasant .....

plumber .....

police .....

portion .....

postman .....

potential .....

precious .....

predominate .....

preference .....

preferential .....

premises .....

premium .....

presentation .....

Prime Minister .....

principles .....

priority .....

problem .....

professionally .....

profit margin .....

pro-forma .....

programmes .....

progression .....

project .....

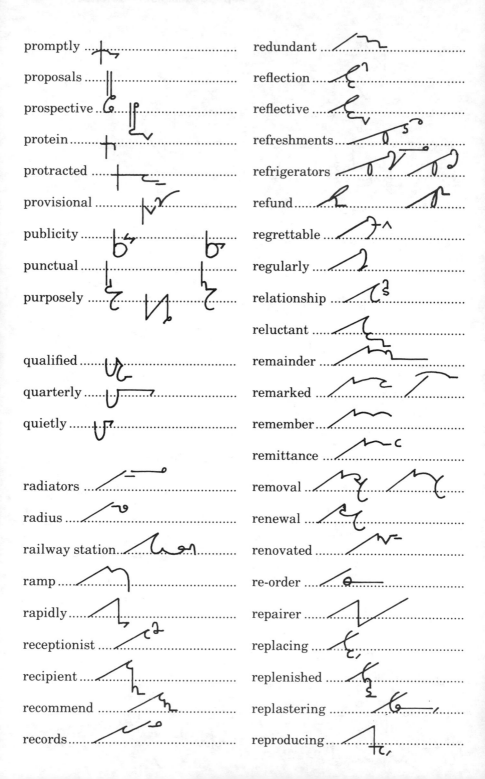

promptly	redundant
proposals	reflection
prospective	reflective
protein	refreshments
protracted	refrigerators
provisional	refund
publicity	regrettable
punctual	regularly
purposely	relationship
	reluctant
qualified	remainder
quarterly	remarked
quietly	remember
	remittance
radiators	removal
radius	renewal
railway station	renovated
ramp	re-order
rapidly	repairer
receptionist	replacing
recipient	replenished
recommend	replastering
records	reproducing

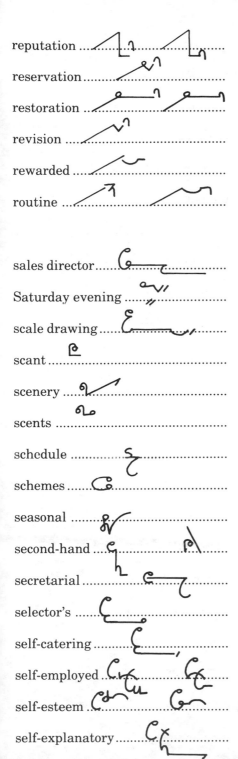

reputation

reservation

restoration

revision

rewarded

routine

sales director

Saturday evening

scale drawing

scant

scenery

scents

schedule

schemes

seasonal

second-hand

secretarial

selector's

self-catering

self-employed

self-esteem

self-explanatory

semi-precious

serenity

serious consideration

sessions

shareholders

shortage

shortly

short-sighted

signature

similarly

simply

sincerely

slowly

smuggler

solicitor's

specialist

specialized

spread

stable

standard of living

state of affairs

statutory

steroid

Stonehenge ....

straight away ....

strawberry ....

strenuous ....

stressful ....

strongly ....

studios ....

subsequent ....

substantial ....

successful ....

suddenly ....

sufferers ....

sugar ....

suit ....

suitable ....

supermarket ....

supervised ....

supposedly ....

surplus ....

switchboard ....

sympathetically ....

table-tennis ....

take part ....

tastefully ....

technology ....

teenagers ....

telephone conversation ....

telephone number ....

telephonist ....

temptation ....

thank you for your enquiry ....

thank you for your letter ....

the other day ....

theatre ....

theses ....

this letter ....

thorough ....

thousands of people ....

thousands of years ago ....

throughout ....

time-consuming ....

to say ....

together with ....

top drawer ....

torrential ....

towards the ....

trade-in ....

trampolining ....

transfusion ....

travellers' cheques ....

treasurer ....

tremendously ....

unanimously ....

unaware ....

underfelt ....

undertaken ....

under-use ....

unexpected ....

unfortunately ....

union ....

unit ....

unsightly ....

unsatisfactory ....

unusual ....

up-market ....

upright ....

upward ....

urgent ....

urgently ....

useful ....

usually ....

utility ....

vacancy ....

vehicle ....

version ....

very soon ....

very well ....

video recorder ....

vocabulary ....

voluntary ....

wallpaper ....

we were pleased ....

we were very sorry ....

well stocked ....

whether or not ....

whichever ....

whirlwind ....

wide-angle ....

wildlife ....

windscreen ....

withdraw ....

with reference to your letter ....

wondering ....

woodworm ....

word processors ....

workforce ....

worthwhile ....

youngsters ....

your company ....